Fresh Voices from the Periphery

YOUTHFUL PERSPECTIVES OF MINORITIES 100 YEARS AFTER TRIANON

Edited by Susan M. Papp, Ph.D.

Copyright © 2021 Rakoczi Foundation — www.studentswithoutboundaries.org

All rights reserved. No part of this publication may be reproduced or transmitted in any form or by any means, electronic or mechanical, including photocopying, recording, or any information storage and retrieval system, except for brief quotations in books, reviews, or articles, without permission, in writing, from the editor.

Published in 2021 by Kinetics Design, KDbooks.ca

ISBN 978-1-988360-67-6 (paperback)

ISBN 978-1-988360-68-3 (ebook)

Editors: Susan M. Papp, Ph.D, with Katalin Kálmán Hajdók and Zoltán Csadi

Project Manager: Eloise Lewis, www.lifetales.ca

Design concept and illustrations: Gábor Édes, www.gaboredes.com

Cover and interior design, typesetting, online publishing and printing:
Daniel Crack, Kinetics Design, KDbooks.ca, linkedin.com/in/kdbooks/
Printed in Canada

CONTENTS

Preface   7
    Dr. Susan M. Papp

Introduction   12
    Dr. Emőke J.E. Szathmáry, CM, OM, Ph.D, FRSC

Historical Background: What Happened in 1920?   24
    Dr. Ádám Suslik

PART ONE   OUTCASTS   33

"Where Did You Learn to Speak Hungarian So Well?"   34
    Tibor Bálint

Past and Present in the Foothills of the Carpathians   37
    Tibor Gyöngyössy

The Value of Our Traditions   40
    Virág Júlia Iszlai

"Torn Away" from a Transcarpathian Perspective   43
    Júlia Kovács

National Identity Is Boundless   46
    Vivien Marti

Our Life   49
    Hanna Peresztegi

A Nation of Survivors   52
    Tamás R. Benedek

This Is My Home   55
    Norbert Bence

The Role of Faith   58
    Réka Baricz

Transcarpathia: The Centre of My Heart   60
    Genovéva Svingola

PART TWO   SEARCHING FOR A WAY ON THE PERIPHERY   63

Historical Musings   65
    Johanna Baróthi

Thoughts on Happiness from the South — 68
Natália Gulyás Oldal

It Seemed to Be Only a Signature, Yet It Sealed Fates — 70
Teodóra Gyurkó

How Much Longer? — 73
Evelin Kitti Hidi

The One Hundred Years of Solitude of Trianon — 76
Dr. Ilona Kotolácsi Mikóczy

Hungarians Without Borders — 80
Attila Norbert Ferenc

On an Undertaking — 83
Dr. Zsuzsanna Napsugár Tóth

Let Us Never Forget to Remember! — 86
Máté Marton

On the Margins of Trianon — 89
Arnold Mészáros

Let Us Be an Example of Unity — 92
Izabella Nagy

Thoughts on a Collective European Future — 95
Nóémi Tatár Jakab

What Is the Key to Our Survival? — 98
Klaudia Varga

PART THREE   WE ARE THE FUTURE! — 101

Trianon 100 — Past, Present, Future — 103
Réka Antal

The Winds of Change after the Storm of Trianon — 106
Orsolya Bálint

The Road to Acceptance — 109
Ágnes Fekete

My Trianon — 112
Ágota Regina Hidi

The Key to Our Survival — 114
Éva Andrea Kántor

Questions on the Eternal Existence of a Nation   117
Réka Kelemen

With Unbroken Faith   120
Árpád Konnát

A Contemporary Nation that Is Surrounded by Itself   123
Erika Ködöböcz

How to Proceed Despite the Common Past   127
Emőke László

I Smile at the World Because of Who I Am!   130
Krisztina Magosi

Nurturing Our Roots   132
Kinga Noémi Mezey

An Identity Encoded in the Spirit   135
Emilia Peleskei

Homework for a Lifetime   138
Enikő Sőreg

Heaven and Earth, Saint and Sinner, or Our Twentieth Century, Our Trianon   141
Dr. Erzsébet Fanni Tóth

PART FOUR   CANADIAN VOICES   **145**

Using the Past to Build a Stronger Future   147
András Z. Diósady

Adapting to Change   154
Karoline Farkas

The Bittersweet Joys of Teen Miscommunication   158
Dr. Katherine Magyarody

The Importance of Resilience   167
Mária Horváth

Being Empowered   171
Mónika Borbély

Finding Identity   174
Tamás Gáspár

ACKNOWLEDGEMENTS   Dr. Susan M. Papp   179

> We are in this world
> so that we will be at home
> in it somewhere.
>
> — ÁRON TAMÁSI

Fresh Voices from the Periphery

PREFACE

Dr. Susan M. Papp

THIS book is evidence that history matters. History is not only the study of the past — it is also the examination of how events of the past have impacted lives in the present. You are holding in your hands a collection of thought-provoking essays written by young people whose families have lived as minorities in various countries in east-central Europe for four generations. They became minorities not because their families migrated to different parts of Europe, but because the borders were changed over their heads. Today, these Hungarian minorities live in Transylvania in Romania, southern Slovakia, Transcarpathia in Ukraine, and Vojvodina in Serbia.

Until 1920, their regions and communities were part of Hungary. Following the end of the First World War, the victorious nations broke up empires and mapped out new successor states. Through the Treaty of Trianon, one of the treaties drafted at that time, the victorious nations sought to create new nation-states, but they created multi-ethnic states with large minority populations. Hungarian minorities were part of this dictated peace.

The essays contained in this volume were submitted through an online competition held by the Rákoczi Foundation of Canada in May 2020. The title of the call for essays was simply: "What does Trianon mean to you today?" The response was overwhelming. Within a brief span of thirty days, there were almost one hundred essays and five short films submitted from students and young professionals who have lived for most or all of their developmental years as minorities in the above-mentioned countries. Some respondents are university students, while others have completed their degrees and are working professionals.

Some still live in the countries where they were born, others have left in search of educational and career opportunities in the European Union.*

Since 1994, the Rákoczi Foundation of Canada has sponsored a program called Students Without Boundaries for students living in minority status in east-central Europe. The program was founded as borders were re-opening following the collapse of communism. These minorities were the forgotten minorities of Europe. The topic of Hungarian minorities fell into a category of historical memory that, following the Second World War, both in the east and west, European nations willingly submerged into the "freezer of history," meaning that talking about it was forbidden. Since the collapse of the Soviet Union and other significant geopolitical changes that have unfolded in Europe since 1989, a much-debated "revival of memory" has occurred.

Until the early 1990s, these young people living in minority status rarely had the opportunity to travel outside their towns and villages, let alone outside their country of birth. The motivation behind the founding of the program was that the organizers believed they could make a difference in bringing Canadian ideals of multiculturalism and tolerance to a region of east-central Europe so frequently divided by ethnic divisions and misinformation. Students Without Boundaries became an educational exchange program as more and more Canadian students also took part and learned about the everyday lives of these minorities.

Since 1994, more than 3,500 students from Slovakia, Romania, Ukraine, Serbia, Canada, and the United States have taken part in this international student educational exchange program. The targeted age group — fourteen through eighteen — is seen as the most sensitive period in the formation of one's identity and self-esteem. Culturally specific ways of gender identity are among the first that most people encounter, along with ethnic identity. Identity negotiation is a dynamic process. Culturally specific assumptions, contained within a diverse range of interrelated practices (such as language, religion, and sexuality, among others), mean that a person's identity is multi-dimensional.

---

* This paper, Historical Reflections: Collective Memory through the Lens of Minority Communities, was presented at a conference organized by the Centre for European, Russian, and Eurasian Studies at the Munk School for Global Affairs and Public Policy at the University of Toronto by Dr. Papp on October 15, 2020.

This is especially true for young people living in minority status, as they face the challenges of being accepted in both the minority community as well as in the majority community. It is a feature of belonging to a minority group to try to understand others, as well as oneself, who one is, and where one belongs. A healthy self-identity is important to lead a stable, well-balanced life, and Students Without Boundaries assists students in finding their places in the world. There is no need to explain ethnic identity to participants; this is already an integral part of their lives. There is a need, however, to encourage them to be able to accept this part of their identity and at the same time, to also be open to understanding other cultures. Students Without Boundaries provides a framework for self-exploration within the context of their own reality.

Because the program widens the horizons of these young people, the majority of the participants are later propelled into careers they would otherwise not even have considered. They learn about scholarships, bursaries, and other educational exchange programs, such as the Erasmus program for university students within the European Union. The Canadian voices/writers demonstrate that they have gained a deeper understanding of minority rights/human rights through their participation in the Students Without Boundaries program. Through taking part, they obtained valuable insights on what it means to live in minority status in east-central Europe.

As a historian and filmmaker, I've always been interested in the frequently discussed sociological term "trans-generational transmission of trauma," the passing down of traumatic events from one generation to another. I dealt with this topic extensively in my first independently directed film, *Debris of War*, about the ordeals faced by Bosnian refugees who had to flee for their lives in the former war-torn Yugoslavia.

The call for essays by the Rákóczi Foundation elicited a strong response from these young people because of the foundation's outstanding work in the region through the Students Without Boundaries program. The idea to publish these essays was prompted by the inspiring writings submitted by the authors. Through the first twenty-six years of the program's existence, hundreds of donors — both individual and corporate from Canada, the United States, Israel, the European Union and other countries around the world — have generously provided financial resources to sustain the program. To list them all would take up many pages in this volume. However, Andrew Heinemann and family deserve special thanks for their outstanding support. Many of these donors experienced the feeling of being "outcast" at some point in their development. As benefactors, they wanted to ensure that young people living in the regions would not go through similar experiences as they had endured during their own developmental years.

Many donated not just financially, but substantially in other ways as well. Yitzhak Livnat (Sándor Weisz, a.k.a. Suti), a Holocaust survivor, born in Nagyszöllős (today: Vinogradjiv, Ukraine), was, along with his family, deported to Auschwitz/Birkenau in 1944. Each year, for over twenty years, he travelled to Budapest to meet the student participants to provide his first-hand account of what happened to him when he was fifteen years old.

Thanks to the Board of Directors of the Rákoczi Foundation for their support in bringing this volume to completion. Special thanks to Professor Emőke Szathmáry, President Emeritus of the University of Manitoba, for her deeply insightful introduction. Thanks also to Professor Levente Diósady, Robert Austin, Director of the Hungarian Studies Program at the University of Toronto, and Professor András Ludányi for their valued advice and support. The work of Zoltán Csadi and Katalin Kálmán Hajdók, in reading, assessing and copy editing, was outstanding. Thanks also goes to Ildikó Csermely, Balázs Csibi, Andrew Diósady, Tibor Lukács, Dr. Éva Tömöry, and Zsuzsanna Tóthfalusy. Peter Csermely and Mária Máté completed excellent work in translating the essays.

Last but not least, a debt of gratitude is owed to William Béla Aykler and his wife, Zsuzsa, founders of the Students Without Boundaries program, whose persistence and dedication grew the program to what it is today.

In 2008, Students Without Boundaries was awarded the first **Charlemagne Youth Prize by the European Parliament** for promoting tolerance and integration and creating a long-term network of support for these minorities. This volume is part of the ongoing effort to bring the views of these young people to the forefront, to let their voices be heard. They write about the challenges of living on the periphery of the countries in which they live, about the many aspects of still waiting to belong, after one hundred years, and for educational and career opportunities.

Their fresh voices and views are important in bridging the gap of misunderstandings, and in healing the wounds. These writings are critical for historians, sociologists, ethnologists, and those concerned about the fate of these regions to gain a deeper understanding of how this generation of young people, representing the fourth generation in their families who have lived in minority status in these countries, perceive the Treaty of Trianon that changed the lives of their families and their communities so dramatically one hundred years ago. Their voices offer distinctive perspectives and demonstrate that historical events, and the issue of minorities cannot be paved over or placed into the freezer of history. The politics of discrimination and treatment of these minorities as second-class citizens simply cannot be allowed to continue. Their voices must be heard.

Susan M. Papp, Ph.D.

Susan M. Papp has had a distinguished career as an award-winning broadcaster and filmmaker. One of her documentaries received the prestigious Michener Award for Public Service. Dr. Papp is the author of several books and many scholarly articles, including a history of the Munk-Munkácsi family in the volume *How it Happened: Documenting the Tragedy of Hungarian Jewry*. One of her books, *Outcasts: A Love Story*, is based on a true story that took place during the Holocaust. Originally written in English, *Outcasts* has been translated into three languages and made into a documentary film. Susan Papp earned her Ph.D. in Modern European History from the University of Toronto. Her dissertation, *The Politics of Exclusion and Retribution in the Hungarian Film Industry, 1929–1947*, is presently being prepared for publication. She is President of the Rákóczi Foundation of Canada.

INTRODUCTION

Dr. Emőke J.E. Szathmáry, CM, OM, Ph.D, FRSC
President Emeritus, University of Manitoba

In my Grade 11 history class, some sixty years ago, Fr. Mazerolle's black cassock was often fringed with puffs of chalk dust, as he beat a staccato rhythm on the board, punctuating each carefully uttered word: Every war has causes, and every peace treaty has consequences — political, economic, social! The history of armed conflicts is formally taught in schools and universities, past battles are analyzed through formal lenses in books and scholarly journals, and old newspapers carry stories revealing the truth of what occurred in "our times." Except that, the victors and the vanquished of a war tend to have different understandings of the facts, and those differences can generate debates about the veracity of claimed causes, as well as the justice and fairness of the consequences.

This book is grounded in an event that occurred a hundred years ago, but its essays focus not on the still-ongoing debates and judgments of historians, politicians, and journalists. Its focus is on the consequences of the Treaty of Trianon as experienced and expressed by young people, a few still in their teens, and most others in the early stages of their adult lives. Thirty-eight of the essays in this book, comprising its "Fresh Voices from the Periphery," were written by the grandchildren and great-grandchildren of Hungarians who, on the morning of June 5, 1920, woke up in a designated country other than Hungary, where they had gone to bed. Another six essays, the "Canadian Voices," were written by descendants of those who woke on Hungarian soil on that day but chose to leave it in the aftermaths of the wars or revolutions of the twentieth century. All had taken part at one time or another in the Students Without Boundaries program of the Rákóczi Foundation, which, through its scholarships, promotes Canadian values such as multiculturalism and the virtue of tolerance in pluralistic societies. Their stories put a human face on the persistence of identity and national consciousness, their narratives breathe life into the meaning of being together and apart. Reflection on their struggles to belong inevitably raises questions about possibilities for reconciliation between majority and minority members of the societies in which they are embedded.

The pivotal event that forms the background to the commentaries in this book is the Treaty of Trianon, which was signed on June 4, 1920, and formally ended the First World War between the Allied and Associated Powers and the Kingdom of Hungary. Many Canadians are aware of treaties between North American Indigenous peoples and invading Europeans, among them the Great Peace of Montreal, signed in 1701 between representatives of New France and those of the Haudenosaunee (Iroquois) Confederacy, as well as the Treaties of Peace and Neutrality that were negotiated between several North American Indigenous peoples and the British Crown before Canadian Confederation. It is worth noting, therefore, that the Treaty of Trianon was not negotiated, but was dictated by the Allies. Adam Suslik, Ph.D., a young historian from the Periphery, provides readers with a succinct overview of the territorial demands of existing and newly created states around Hungary before the signing of this treaty, and the consequences of Trianon for Hungary and Hungarians thereafter. These included the dissolution of the thousand-year-old kingdom of Hungary, as well as transfers of more than two-thirds of its territory and about one-third of its population to other countries. Those transferred, including three million ethnic Hungarians — my four grandparents among them — had no choice in these matters. Their one option was to choose between abandoning their homes and relocating within the new borders of a truncated Hungary or remaining where they were and being deemed members of other sovereign states.

The socio-economic consequences of the new border placements were crippling for Hungary, and the callous treatment of Hungarians generated outrage and hostility among them. Hungarian resentment of Trianon has persisted for a century, so it should not be surprising that the states that received the fruits of Hungary's partition remain wary that a redrawing of borders in favour of Hungary might be attempted. That such action could be done peacefully is inconceivable and, as Dr. Suslik notes, Hungarians, regardless of where they reside, have just "one option for continued existence: peace, solidarity, and cooperation with neighbouring nations."

Trianon sealed the fate of Hungary and its people, but Hungarians have not disappeared from the regions transferred to other sovereign states. What is the key to their cultural survival a century after the Treaty of Trianon? Would the opinions of young ethnic Hungarians in these regions, based on their lived experiences, provide insights, not just locally but more broadly, within Europe? As the editor of this volume, Dr. Susan Papp, details in her preface, the Rákóczi Foundation issued a call for essays, and this volume contains the unvarnished views of young people born and raised in Slovakia, Ukraine (Transcarpathia), Romania (Transylvania), and Serbia (Vojvodina), as well as those in Canada. Their desire to know about their roots binds them, but the experiences of those who remained on the lands of their ancestors stand in stark contrast to those who grew to adulthood on Canadian soil. Are there lessons to be learned from all this?

I had asked to read the essays from the "Periphery" — the regions from the Midwestern, Eastern, and Southern Carpathian Mountains that were transferred to other states — in the Hungarian language first. Subsequently, I read them in English also, because I feared errors in the translations. My time was well spent, because I found that the translations are excellent, and their substantive and emotional impacts are strong. Even so, in my native language, the essays struck a much deeper chord of resonance than they did in English, the language in which I am educated, in which my daily life proceeds, and in which I am significantly more proficient. The difference I perceived is a testament to the adage that much is lost in translation. Linguists have long argued that language influences how we perceive the world, in part because there is a relationship between the spoken or written word and the culture those words reflect — the shared beliefs, histories, social behaviours, and lifeways of a people. There is a Hungarian proverb which encapsulates this linkage: *"Ahány nyelv, annyi ember,"* which is translated colloquially as "You are as many people as the languages you speak." I am writing in English, and I will therefore leave to readers of English to discern not just the layered meanings of Trianon to each author, but also an appreciation of the issues that lie at the heart of cultural survival in a multi-ethnic world. My own focus is on what the essays reveal collectively, both explicitly and implicitly. Other readers' interpretations may differ from mine, but I trust we would find common ground in what it would take for young people living on the Periphery to realize their hopes for their individual and collective futures.

All the essays from the Periphery address the designated topic but they are aggregated under three distinct headings, as Parts I, II, and III. The title of each part indicates the predominant theme that emerged from the essays in the given section, a theme stated overtly in some compositions and less so in others. The three themes also follow a logical order, comparable to a map that describes the start of a route, its tentative course, and the desired destination.

Part One, "Outcasts," contains ten essays, and its title is appropriate. All the authors state that keeping their language and their Hungarian cultural consciousness is of paramount importance to them. At the same time several are explicit about not belonging, and their tone is tinged with bitterness. Their feelings of exclusion arise from actions directed against them as members of the Hungarian minority in the countries where they were born. For some, "not belonging" refers not just to one's birthplace but also to the "mother land," Hungary. While being regarded as an outsider is hard enough to deal with in the country of one's birth, it may be most painful when experienced on visits to Hungary. In the latter, those from the Periphery are regarded — at best — as hyphenated Hungarians (e.g., Slovak-Hungarian), with precedence given to membership in the foreign nation, thereby diminishing, if not invalidating, the ethnic identity to which the visitors cling. In the countries of their births, they are either labelled in reverse (e.g., Hungarian-Serb), which indicates that one is not an authentic member of the given nation-state, or, more typically, by their ethnic minority origin only (Magyar), which marks them as foreign in that nation-state. In these essays, the retelling of the Trianon-mandated transfers of territory and people to other nations becomes a prelude to the current mistreatment of these Hungarian minorities. Cumulatively, this becomes a matter-of-fact background noise, an accumulation of small indignities, frank public insults, attempts by members of majority groups to obliterate memory by the defacement of historic Hungarian monuments and outright discrimination against Hungarians in employment, even when they are fluent in the majority's language. One has the sense that resignation about injustice in the past and prejudicial treatment in the present is paired closely with a muted anger. Defiance is present, outrage also, especially about recent legislation in Ukraine and Slovakia that disallows education in any other language than that of the majority in each nation-state.

Belonging — acceptance as a member of a community — is validation of one's authentic self. For these young people, belonging requires freedom to speak and to learn in Hungarian, and to practise Hungarian customs and traditions. Some express a deep affiliation with the transferred lands of their births, rather than with the nation-state that now controls those lands. Each essay concludes either by stating actions that would facilitate a continued Hungarian presence in the transferred territories or by expressing faith that their communities there will endure.

Part Two, "Searching for a Way on the Periphery," contains twelve essays, with an equal number from each of Slovakia, Ukraine, Romania, and Serbia. The editor has grouped them under a heading that indicates activity to identify a desired action, without identifying the best action among several proposed. As expected, there is significant overlap between these essays and those in Part I. Unanimity remains regarding the need to preserve ethnic identity and to maintain Hungarian heritage, for which education in the Hungarian language, and usage of this language in daily life, is essential. Similarly, the authors express a profound desire to ensure their community's continuity in the lands where they were born. After all, as one author remarked, they have not moved, just the locations of the borders were changed. However, in several essays the examples presented to illustrate local situations are more detailed, more intense, and what is noted as required to address discrimination is also more explicit than in Part I. From these writings a second goal emerges focused not just on eliminating prejudicial treatment, but also on securing basic human rights for ethnic Hungarians as a matter of observed law. The relevant question then is: *how* can that be achieved?

From the perspective of two Transylvanian authors, the way to safeguard Hungarian ethnic identity is through autonomy and self-determination in their homeland. Equally specific are two authors from other transferred regions, who suggest that reconciliation with the majority is the way to achieve this goal. Between these are other essays that propose routes that would perhaps be of more service to the interests of their community than of a single individual. For example, there are essays that stress the importance of obtaining a university education in Hungary or elsewhere in Europe, with the general expectation that educated people would return home to use their skills on behalf of their communities. Other essays produce no clear-cut proposals on what path to follow, but their authors' comments suggest that they are closer to thinking about getting along with the majority group than are others. For example, some acknowledge that learning the majority's language was difficult and slow, but whether hard or easy, they stress that one must become fluent in it. As one author says, in conjunction with a good education, fluency in the majority language would help to develop the self-reliance necessary to direct one's economic and cultural future, rather than waiting for one or another government to act.

It is worth noting that a few essays show awareness that the majority populations in their countries may have inherited negative attitudes toward Hungarians from their ancestors, who remembered ill treatment when the transferred territories were still under Hungarian control. Realizing that there are three sides to a coin may be a necessary skill for re-examining the trans-generational impact of memories in zones of ethnic discord. Change begins by listening to other people's points of view, and typically there are more than two. Those who identify reconciliation as the means to maintain Hungarian consciousness in their homelands by developing better relations with majority group members emphasize the need to see merit in different points of view.

The fourteen essays in Part Three, "We Are the Future!" have a different tone than the earlier ones. Trianon's impact is certainly understood, but its burden does not mean to the essayists that the current generation should be frozen into a past that is irreconcilable with the desired future. Unanimity remains about the biggest imperative — preservation of Hungarian language and Hungarian culture in the authors' homelands — though some differences remain about the method to be employed to achieve this. One essayist points to the need for members of the community to hold together, and cease making judgments that deem one person a better Hungarian than the next. Another suggests that modernization of the received Hungarian idiom in arts and in music would make Hungarian culture more relevant to youth, and this too would enhance cultural preservation. Her suggestions reminded me of the delight I felt when I heard in 1986 the music and lyrics of *István a Király!* (*Stephen the King!*) — a rock musical (of all things!) about King Saint Stephen, Hungary's first king. Others emphasize that Hungarian consciousness resides within individuals — a matter of spirit, rather than territory — and that spirit of ethnic consciousness can and must be maintained anywhere and everywhere by parents who owe it to their young. Most striking to me was the assertion that the responsibility to maintain a vibrant Hungarian presence in the authors' homelands is theirs, and requires that they develop understanding with the majority community. Getting to know each other in the language of the majority — the language of the state — is a necessary undertaking. What one essayist calls "peaceful coexistence" and another, "reconciliation" are actions that require acceptance of differences between mismatched ethnic groups and enable them, at minimum, to tolerate each other. The authors of these fourteen essays do have different opinions about ways to solve their common minority-status dilemma, but overall they display confidence, even optimism, by asserting that they can choose to live where their lives will unfold. They will remain rooted in the soil of their ancient homeland, regardless that it was transferred, and they will build their futures as proud Hungarians within the multi-ethnic societies into which they have been born.

Part Four, "Canadian Voices," contains six essays, and they focus on a related but slightly different set of questions than those considered by the writers from the Periphery. The Canadians were asked to consider how their views on minority rights changed after they completed their participation in the Students Without Boundaries program. Did their experiences with minority-group students from Slovakia, Ukraine, Romania, and Serbia alter their views on the world, and what impact did those experiences have on their lives since? All six of the essayists were raised in the province of Ontario, Canada, and five of them were also born in southern Ontario. I read the essays in the original Canadian English in which they were written.

The small number of essays in Part Four reflects the significantly smaller pool of Canadians relative to those from the Periphery who have taken part in the Students Without Boundaries summer program. Indeed, one author's involvement began as a group leader rather than as a student participant. The greatest difference among the essays reflects the experience of the writers and the stage of life in which they find themselves. Their greatest similarity indicates the safety and freedom the writers have in which to be their authentic selves, both Canadian and Hungarian.

By discovering how they differed from their companions from the Periphery, the authors came face-to-face with their Canadian-ness, which was manifest in their assumptions, attitudes, and behaviours. At the same time, they recognized their Hungarian-ness, not just by their shared language but also by the realization that, if they were living in any of their companions' home countries, they would bear the same burdens of inequity and prejudicial treatment as did their companions, simply because they are ethnic Hungarians.

The Canadians' perspectives about themselves and their companions were clearly altered by what they heard and saw, and those experiences have reverberated in their lives ever since. Some remark that, in comparison to what their companions grappled with, their own difficulties became insignificant. They admired their companions' resilience in adversity and drew inspiration from it to confront their own problems, to overcome the self-doubts and fears that had blocked them from moving forward in the directions they set for themselves.

Another writer found that his experiences on the Periphery, after the conclusion of the summer program, led him to an unexpected discovery: dual Canadian and Hungarian identities embedded in his personality. It was a Canadian lens through which he viewed the beauty of the natural world, and it was a friendly Hungarian manner, oriented toward others, that governed his social interactions with people and the community. Hearing and directly experiencing prejudice in some places visited on the Periphery led another Canadian to reflect on the meaning of human rights in a broader context, in peoples and places that were known to her in the world. She discerned that human rights are as much the rights of Hungarian minorities in the countries bordering Hungary as they are the rights of Roma in Hungary itself, and the rights of the Indigenous peoples of Canada. To awaken awareness of minority rights among majority-group members, individuals must "walk the talk," instilling where they can respect for human diversity and a desire for justice. For that author, change began by teaching these concepts to her children at home and by discussing them with students attending her classes.

In sum, there is no question that participation in the Students Without Boundaries program changed the perceptions of Canadian young people on the quality of lives led by their counterparts from the transferred lands. In fact, all the participants grew in their appreciation of their common Hungarian heritage and its language. The Canadians, however, also realized that it is easier for them than for their companions to maintain their Hungarian language and identity, because they have freedom to speak Hungarian, including on the streets. Furthermore, participation in Hungarian cultural events does not imperil their safety.

All four parts of this volume contain the thoughtfully rendered, personal views of so many young people! Their essays merit deep reading and contemplation, for each will reveal much more to readers than my summaries allow. My final thoughts return to the reasons why the essays were written and what their authors disclose about the consequences of an old peace treaty on their lives today.

A century after the Treaty of Trianon came into effect, Hungarian identity and Hungarian consciousness still characterize young people drawn from Hungarian minorities in the transferred lands along the arc of the Carpathians. They have not been absorbed into the majority in any of the countries where they were born and raised, and yet their continued presence there is threatened. Essayists from the Periphery, as well as from Canada, note that Hungarian cultural preservation in their multi-ethnic societies requires retention of their language and of a lifestyle that at minimum makes room for participation in Hungarian community life in places of worship, in cultural centres, and through public celebrations of events of Hungarian significance. All the authors are drawn from minority communities, but the marked difference in their lives is linked to their status as minorities in their homelands.

Hungarians are subject to multiple and various forms of oppression in all the lands transferred to other nation-states after Trianon. No doubt there are multiple explanations to justify discriminatory actions in each of these sovereign states, but in my view the simplest will suffice: The very definition of a nation-state, so popular among the designers of the Treaty of Trianon, excludes ethnic minorities. Though the Hungarian minority's presence in the transferred lands was known from the onset, and is acknowledged today, they are not regarded as truly belonging to the nation whose majority constitutes the state in which they live. However, without vigorous actions taken by governments of de facto multi-ethnic rather than nation-states — from enacting and enforcing legislation that guarantees human rights for minorities, to teaching respect for human cultural and biological diversity, to encouraging behaviour on the streets that accepts the human dignity of minority members — some individuals from the majority will act on their assumed precedence and priority in society, disparaging those they regard as less worthy. Inevitably, such acts of prejudice will generate group tensions, and these will rise as the number of repressive actions grows and intensifies. This should matter to governments, because the challenges of prejudice not only constrain individual lives and build internal hostility, but they also prohibit drawing on the strengths of the collective, which could together ensure a multi-ethnic society's secure and thriving future.

In contrast to the situations that exist in the multi-ethnic societies of the Periphery, minorities in Canada are encouraged to preserve their separate identities as they accommodate to Canadian society and build a Canadian identity. A generation ago, diversity was certainly present in Canada, but today it is emphasized, along with equity and inclusivity, as factors that bring richness to Canadian society.

Is it possible for a change in attitude to truly occur? Indeed, it can and has, as shown by Canadians who desire it and promote it, as have their successive governments. After reading many quotable sentences in these essays, one by András Diósady resonates within my memory, evoking an undeniable aspect of Canadian culture: "I have never experienced hatred for being different." I can attest to that too, despite the fact that my name has identified my Hungarian-immigrant origin throughout the seventy years that Canada has been my home.

And yet, Canada and Canadians were not always this way.

Multiculturalism first became federal government policy in 1971 for practical reasons, among them the need to cope with rising Francophone nationalism in the Province of Québec and increasing cultural complexity in the rest of Canada. Since then, however, practicality has given way to a change in the national ethos in matters of fairness and justice, as the reaction to the findings of the Truth and Reconciliation Commission of Canada have shown. In 2015 this Commission documented Canada's past treatment of Indigenous peoples. Foremost in that treatment were methods to extinguish indigenous languages and Indigenous cultural consciousness among several generations of Indigenous children. That a great wrong was done in the past is now acknowledged by all political parties, and the Canadian public. Today a reconciliation process between Indigenous peoples and the descendants of Francophone and Anglophone settlers, as well as newcomers from every continent in the world, is underway. As always, the process of reconciliation begins by listening and finding merit in different points of view. Individuals as well as government can provide remedies required to correct past and current injustices. Each step in such a process increases the likelihood that a fair and equitable culture will be formed to the benefit of all members of society. Cultural change is complex, and portions of such change are works in progress. Nevertheless, the Canadian example shows that enormous shifts in public attitudes and government actions can occur within a lifetime, for these changes have occurred within mine.

Surely, it is worthwhile for the states of east-central Europe to change course in their treatment of minorities. They will find, as Canada has, that their identity is not threatened by other identities manifest in segments of its citizenry. Rather, being safe and free to express all dimensions of one's ethnic identity encourages loyalty to Canada, where respect for cultural diversity and for human dignity are ingrained elements of one's equally cherished Canadian identity. It could also be so for the multi-ethnic states that inherited sizable minorities of Hungarians with the Treaty of Trianon, as attested to by the essays in this volume. Acceptance of multiple ethnic identities among citizens of a country, as in Canada today, simply strengthens the state itself.

In closing, I express my gratitude to the Rákóczi Foundation for its creation and support of the Students Without Boundaries program, which was not known to me until the editor, Dr. Papp, asked me to write an introduction to this volume. The Foundation's support has made it possible for readers to know how the lives of young people living in east-central Europe today have been impacted by decisions made a century ago. Their essays show that they need two fundamental elements in their lives: preservation of their Hungarian language and culture in the countries in which they were born and raised, and acceptance into the mainstream of those countries. In such societies they will be able to build meaningful futures. May the young people from the Periphery discover that their voices have begun a shift in attitudes toward them. May their Canadian counterparts impress on the world that holding on to their Hungarian heritage has made Canada stronger. Respect for human dignity and human rights will make every country stronger. The Atlantic Ocean separates the heirs of Trianon in Canada and those on the Periphery of their "mother country," but their Hungarian heritage binds them. They are apart but not alone.

Emőke J.E. Szathmáry, CM, OM, Ph.D, FRSC
President Emeritus, University of Manitoba

Emőke J.E. Szathmáry is a biological anthropologist whose career combined research, teaching, administration, and community service. She served 12 years as President and Vice-Chancellor of The University of Manitoba. Earlier she was Provost and Vice-President (Academic) at McMaster University, and before that, Dean of Social Science at Western University. She Is a Fellow of the Royal Society of Canada, and a Member of the Order of Canada, and the Order of Manitoba.

Dr. Szathmáry's focus on the genetics of the indigenous peoples of North America included research on the causes of type-2 diabetes, the genetic relationships within and between North American and Siberian peoples, and the microevolution of subarctic populations. Her field research involved Ottawa, Ojibwa and Tlicho peoples in Ontario and the Northwest Territories. She has published over 90 scientific articles and reviews, and co-edited four books. As well she served terms as Editor-in-Chief of the *Yearbook of Physical Anthropology* (1987–91), and the *American Journal of Physical Anthropology* (1995–2001).

HISTORICAL BACKGROUND: WHAT HAPPENED IN 1920?

Dr. Ádám Suslik

For Hungarians, Trianon is an eternal and undigestable trauma, more impactful than the Battle of Mohács, which was lost to the armies of the Ottoman Empire and led to 150 years of Turkish occupation. It was more serious than the losses of the Second World War and the following forty-four years of Soviet occupation. As a historian, I have spent a great deal of time on the period preceding Trianon and the consequences of the peace diktat. As a Hungarian "from across the border," I experienced in my own life the traumatic effects of this event, which took place one hundred years ago but spanned generations. I will try to approach the topic by laying out the historical facts and connections and attempting to state my thoughts as to what led to the dismemberment of historical Hungary and what were Trianon's social and cultural consequences.

Before the decision to go to war took place, Hungary was part of the dualist Austro-Hungarian Empire (where the ministries of finance, foreign affairs, and war were joint only after 1867). On July 28, 1914, Hungary drifted into a war that lasted four and a half years and caused irreparable losses. Hungarian soldiers fought on the endless steppes of Russia and Galicia, the snow-covered Carpathians, and the valley of the Úz River, in the Alps and along the Isonzo River. By the time the armistice was signed in Padua on November 3, 1918, the monarchy existed only on paper. The newly emerged countries had firm hopes that the Entente would give them all the military, economic, and political assistance necessary to make their aspirations come true. The neighbouring states not only gained important industrial and agricultural areas but also vital railway lines.

The cost in human life — those dead, wounded, and captured

— exceeded several million. The peace conferences began in Paris in January of 1919, but the Hungarian delegation, led by Count Albert Apponyi, was allowed to arrive only on January 6, 1920. Hungary, as a defeated nation, was not invited to take part in the discussions; it was only asked to attend immediately before the signing of the treaty and handed a finished document. The American and British plans would have been substantially more favourable to Hungary, as the Americans would have left two-thirds of the Hungarian-populated zones along the border — the British half of the zone — but the new neighbouring states demanded more, and their arguments found receptive ears. The Hungarian delegation was handed the final text of the dictated peace on May 6, 1920. Czechoslovakia was given 61,000 square kilometres, with a population of 3.5 million, of which 30 percent were Hungarians; Romania 103,000 square kilometres and 5.2 million people (31 percent Hungarian) and the Kingdom of Serbs-Croats-Slovenes 20,000 square kilometres and 1.5 million people (30 percent Hungarian). Even Austria, also a defeated country, received Burgenland to ensure the food supply of its large cities and avoid the possibility of Anschluss, the unification of Austria and Germany, which many Austrians wanted. The treaty was signed on June 4, 1920, which did not bring (the hoped-for) peace, but rather defined the future direction of Hungary's foreign-policy efforts, as a result of which Hungary unavoidably drifted into the Second World War on the side of Germany.

Beginning in 1920, around 350,000 to 400,000 ethnic Magyars, mostly intellectuals, left their former homes in the partitioned regions and resettled in Hungary. The majority of these people wanted to live in the capital, Budapest, which was now more important than previously, but Budapest did not have the resources to look after this influx, so the refugees had to wait, and live in boxcars until their fortunes improved. Of the registered refugees, 57 percent came from Romania, and 30 percent from Czechoslovakia. Widespread unemployment, terrible hardship, and inflation continued to be felt for a long time, not to mention the loss of territory.

Trianon changed everything, not only the borders but the economy, the transit of goods, and the traffic networks. All the roads and railways running parallel to the border ended up on the other side of the new borders, mainly for military and economic reasons, like the road and railway network running between Arad [Arad, Romania], Nagyvárad

[Oradea], and Szatmárnémeti [Satu Mare]. The majority of smaller, mostly local, rail networks were cut in half — in the case of Temesköz [Banat] region, into three — by the twisting border. Here, the victors shared the railroad three ways among themselves, exchanging areas. Inexplicably, they severed the major railway line running from Budapest through Szeged, Nagykikinda [Kikinda], Temesvár [Timişoara], and Orsova [Orşova] to Bucharest. The three countries: Czechoslovakia, Romania, and Serbia, demanded the almost purely Hungarian-populated strip of Nagyszöllős [Sevljus, then Czechoslovakia, today Ukraine], Szatmár [Satu Mare, Romania], Nagykároly [Carei], Érmihályfalva [Valea lui Mihai], Nagyvárad [Oradea], Nagyszalonta [Salonta, Arad], apart from the territory left to Hungary, to ensure a strategic land bridge in case of future military action. In the territory left by Trianon, the remaining railway network shrank to 8,671 kilometres from the previous almost 22,000 kilometres. Of the road and highway network — the development of which was important to reach the peripheries of Greater Hungary — a mere 26.2 percent was left by the peace treaty. Of the railway lines, 37.9 percent remained, and of the railway rolling stock, barely a quarter. Of the 6,011 kilometres of navigable waterways, Hungary was left with 2,128 kilometres, those navigable by steamships dropped from 2,511 kilometres to 1,063 kilometres.

An even worse disaster befell Hungarian education and culture. Until 1912, there were four universities in the Kingdom of Hungary: one in Zagreb, two in Budapest (one humanities and one technical/engineering), and one in Kolozsvár (1872). With increased demand, two new universities were set up before 1912, in Debrecen and Pozsony. These universities were staffed by such brilliant minds as Dr. Frigyes Korányi (internal medicine and pulmonary medicine), Donát Bánki (inventor of the carburetor), and Loránd Eötvös (gravitational and surface tension), who in 1895 had founded an intellectual stronghold, the Eötvös College. Separate institutions were devoted to young students who wished to work in agriculture. In 1899, the Veterinary College of Budapest was founded, and future mining and forestry engineers were taught in Selmecbánya [Banská Štiavnica, Czechoslovakia].

Trianon caused Hungary to become a truncated country, with its area reduced from 282,000 square kilometres to 93,000, its population reduced from 18.2 million to 7.6 million, and the majority of universities and technical colleges ended up on the other side of the new borders.

Two-thirds of the colleges and almost half of the high schools were to be found in the annexed territories. Franz Joseph University moved from Kolozsvár [Cluj-Napoca, Romania] to Szeged, and Elizabeth University of Pozsony [Bratislava, Slovakia] relocated to Pécs.

In the political and alliance system of the day, Trianon could not have been avoided, only delayed. There were no allies with whom Hungary had fostered friendly relations (Germany, Turkey, Bulgaria), as they were all on the losing side, or who, in the hopes of grabbing large areas of territory, changed sides just before the end of the war to the winning side (Italy, Romania). There were no supporters who took Hungary's side at the peace conference. This was also unavoidable, because no one saw a need in east-central Europe for a strong country surrounded by Slavic states. Rather the need was for several, smaller countries in alliance with each other, seeking the Entente's favours, and who, in the interest of their continued independence, were ready for immediate military action. The primary goal was to stop the spread of Soviet Communist ideas and prevent the resurgence of Germany. It was feared that Austria, with Hungary or without, would again become allied with Germany.

Since 1920, a number of geographical and political changes have taken place, which have affected the fate of Hungarian minorities in the countries to which they were annexed after the First World War.

The northeastern region was ceded to, and became part of, Czechoslovakia, and was renamed Podkarpatská Rus. The more than 200,000 ethnic Hungarians living there continued to live in peace and harmony with the large numbers of Rusyn, Jewish, and German minorities. This initial evolution was soon brought to a halt by the Second World War, when the region was briefly returned to Hungary. In 1944, the region was placed under Soviet control and, as a result, around 28,000 Hungarians were dragged away to the gulag as collective punishment. Many in this region waited in vain for the return of their fathers, brothers, and sons. But the ordeal was not over. The Soviets nationalized the assets and land of the population, and young men served their military service in the Soviet army. As a result, many hundreds of young Hungarian men fought in Afghanistan (1979 to 1989). In 1991, the Soviet Union ceased to exist, and Transcarpathia became part of independent Ukraine.

The Hungarians of the northern counties ceded to Czechoslovakia initially followed the same path. The 900,000 Hungarians living there formed a significant minority block, however, after the war, the Czechoslovak government stripped them of their citizenship and all rights pertaining to it. During 1946–47, some 44,000 Hungarians were forcibly transported to distant parts of Czechoslovakia for agricultural labour, and several tens of thousands were exiled to or resettled in Hungary because of a forced population exchange. Some easing of conditions was apparent during the socialist era, but as a result of the 1968 Czechoslovak uprising, Soviet troops also took control in this region. With the end of the socialist system in 1993, Czechoslovakia separated into the Czech Republic and Slovakia, with nearly 500,000 Hungarians finding themselves in Slovakia.

Following Trianon, the largest number of Hungarians who found themselves in a minority situation were living in Transylvania and the Partium region in Romania. Their numbers even today reach 1,200,000. The minority rights incorporated into the Treaty of Trianon were never ratified by any Romanian government. Forced and forcible Romanianization was begun in civil administration, as well as in culture. Following the war, many atrocities were committed against this population. The Ceauşescu era saw the beginning of the razing of entire villages, bringing new and more serious hardships to the Hungarian minority, while the Romanian Revolution, which occurred in 1989, swept away another socialist regime.

Hungary's borders were also redrawn along the southern frontier. Vojvodina was given to the Kingdom of Serbia-Croatia-Slovenia (later renamed Yugoslavia after 1929), where around 300,000 declared themselves to be Hungarians. During the Second World War, the partisans carried out large-scale atrocities among the Hungarians, and subsequently forced large numbers to flee. The Hungarians living here also witnessed first-hand the latest conflict, the Balkan wars of the 1990s. Between 1991 and 1992, first Slovenia and Croatia, then Macedonia and Bosnia-Herzegovina, declared their independence. However, the Serbs living there picked up their weapons, and this marked the beginning of a brutal, armed, ethnic conflict. Fear of the war and deprivation again forced thousands of Hungarians to leave their homeland, the land of their birth. To this day, this is the region where the proportion of the Hungarian minority has shown the greatest decrease. The numbers of Hungarians in all these regions have diminished significantly due to deportations, assimilation campaigns, discriminatory laws, and emigration.

Some neighbouring countries to this day dread the prospect (usually around election time) that a time will come when Hungary will demand a return of the annexed territories. However, a responsible national policy cannot support initiatives aimed at the revision of borders. Hungarians, both inside and outside the borders, have only one option for continued existence, and that is peace, solidarity, and co-operation with neighbouring nations. Membership in the European Union, as well as the granting of dual citizenships, means that the majority of the borders have virtually disappeared — with the exception of Serbia and Ukraine. For Hungarians living outside the border, this dual citizenship was a huge psychological and emotional reinforcement, but from the perspective of being able to continue to live in the region of their birth, it also had negative consequences, for the economic crisis started a large-scale emigration.

For Hungarians, I see the key to the continued existence and retention of identity in strong roots, family, and community relations; the nurturing of traditions; and a dedication to common values. The coming generation is faced with a huge task. Amid the challenges of the present and the future they must retain the heritage of their parents and grandparents. As, in my childhood, I had positive experiences (including the Students Without Boundaries program), which nurtured in me the love of my mother tongue and history and a curiosity and tolerance toward other nations, I would like to pass these values on to my children. I find especially important those initiatives through which Hungarian young people, whether living in the capital or in a small village in Transcarpathia, become familiar with the communities in other annexed regions, with their culture, history, and everyday lives. It is important for these groups to meet each other, form living contacts, and have an idea of what it is like to live as a Hungarian in minority status, in a mixed community with other nations.

There is need for openness, change, and compromise on the part of the neighbouring countries, without which living peacefully side-by-side is inconceivable. We must accept that the number of Hungarians living beyond the border will continually diminish as a result of the mass emigration and assimilation of the past one hundred years. Those who leave the land of their birth must not be looked on as enemies but as victims who were forced into making this decision.

Processing the trauma and overcoming difficulties strengthens a person. One hundred years after Trianon, our mission is to face up to the past, and, instead of feeling pain and hate, look into the future. There is no hope that we can change the past, but we can shape the future.

Dr. Ádám Suslik

Ádám Suslik was born in Beregszász [Berehovo, Ukraine] in Transcarpathia.

Currently, Ádám works as a historian in the Hungarian National Archives in Budapest. He received a teacher's diploma in history and geography at the Ferenc Rákóczi II Hungarian College of Transcarpathia in Beregszász. Ádám completed his doctorate in 2017 from the Károli Gáspár Reformed University in historiography. His area of scholarship is focused on the First World War, as well as the Age of Dualism and the interwar period. He has made presentations at a number of conferences, and his research has been published in scientific journals and conference compilations. His first book, co-authored with Árpád Kajon, was *A Monarchia katonája. Schamschula Rezső tábornok élete* [Soldier of the Monarchy: The Life of General Rezső Schamschula] (Magyar Napló, 2019). His second book examined the events of the Hungarian Soviet as it relates to the city of Sopron. As an historian, Ádám has contributed to the production of a six-part documentary film on Trianon. Besides his professional work, he has taken part in countless educational and talent-development programs for younger students. As a student, Ádam participated in the Students Without Boundaries program in 2002. Adam believes the experiences and knowledge he gained, the friendships he made, have greatly influenced him in developing his world view and his identity.

Ádám is working on the publication of the expanded version of his doctoral thesis that deals with the history of Transcarpathia during the First World War.

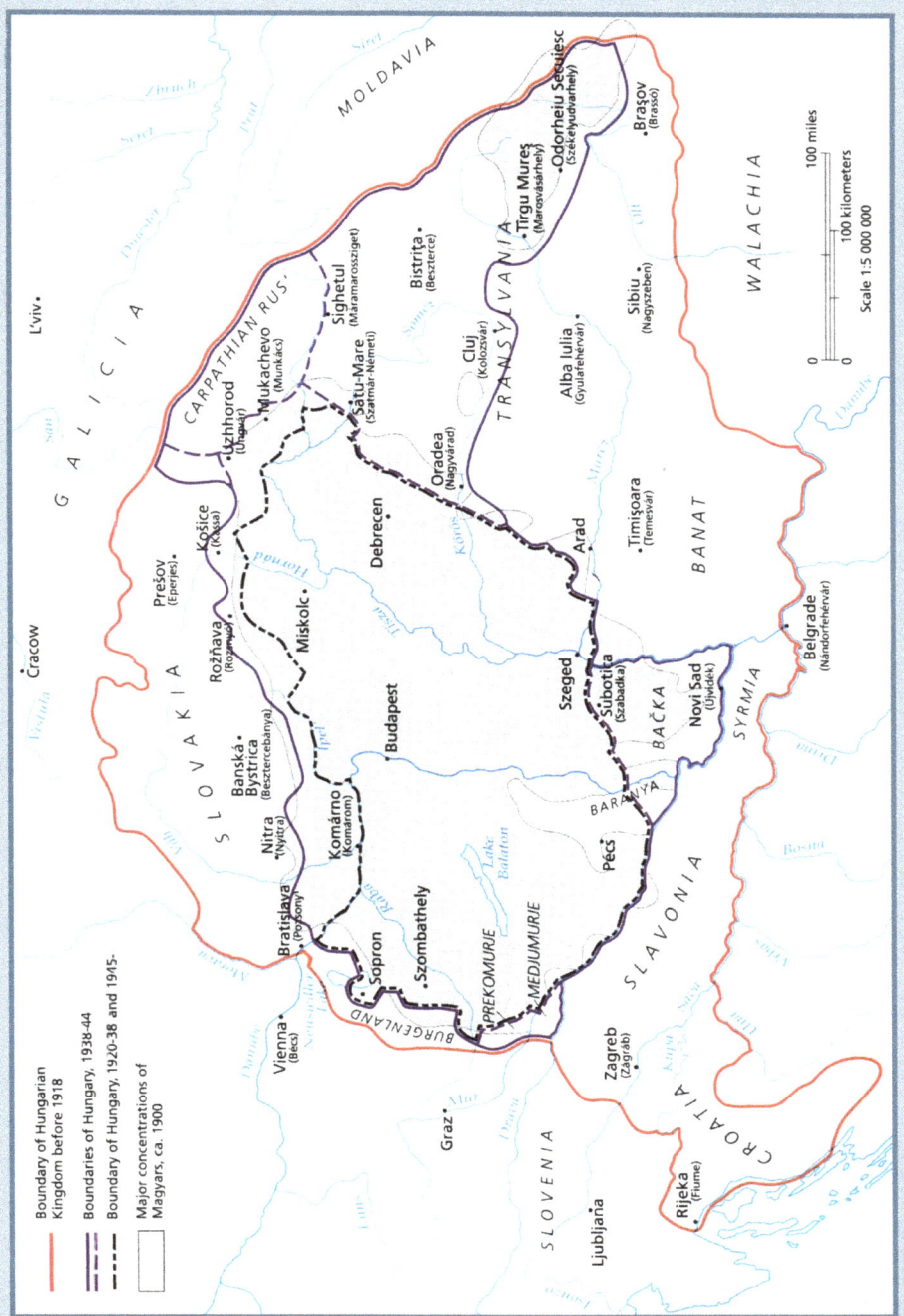

Hungary in the twentieth century. Reproduced from *Historical Atlas of Central Europe* with permission of Paul Robert Magocsi, revised and expanded edition (Seattle: University of Washington Press, 2002).

> A chief attendant of a healthy nation is a national language, because, as long as it survives, the nation lives.
>
> — COUNT ISTVÁN SZÉCHENYI

PART ONE

Outcasts

Le Traité de paix avec la Hongrie sera signé aujourd'hui à Versailles

"WHERE DID YOU LEARN TO SPEAK HUNGARIAN SO WELL?"

Tibor Bálint

As a Hungarian living outside the border of Hungary, I do not feel I can form an objective opinion about the dictated peace of Trianon. At least I cannot. It is interesting to look back on it a century later. My generation was not present when the "Big Ones" committed it to paper, yet we still live in the aftermath and with the attendant consequences. I know everyone has had enough of hearing or reading the sort of news item that pleads for help for the Hungarian communities outside the Hungarian borders, but the reality is that without such support we can't exist.

It is notable that when I stop in Hungary to talk with a local individual, sooner or later we get onto the subject of ancestry, as in "Where are you from?" and I proudly admit to being from Törökbecse [Novi Bečej, Serbia] — which is followed by the usual question: "Where is that?" After I answer, follows one of the most indelicate and hurtful questions: "Where did you learn to speak Hungarian so well?" I have thought long about what would have happened if the dictated peace had not been signed. Then, in my imagination, we would be a part of the mother country, and no one would question my Hungarian-ness, and wouldn't be surprised by how well I speak the language. The biggest problem is that I don't feel at home anywhere! Here, among the Serbs, I will always be a minority. In Hungary, since I attend university there, I will always be a Serbian-Hungarian, or Yugoslav, or even Serb.

But the question remains. What has this to do with Trianon? I grew up in Törökbecse, where we played out in the fields among the ruins of the church of Aracs [Arača, Serbia], while my grandfather checked on the beehives. We spent a lot of time on the street until late evening, my friends and I, Serbs and Hungarians together. But when I entered school, I realized that the world is not black and white as I had seen it. The older children constantly harassed us; a friend was not allowed to go home until he sang the Serb national anthem. We continually asked, "Why is this necessary?" My father is not particularly interested in history. Obviously, he knows about the Conquest, King Saint Stephen, King Mathias, and the Austro-Hungarian Empire, but he is not particularly interested in the revolts of '48 or '56 or the Treaty of Trianon. Feelings of patriotism have been "taught" out of the thinking of his generation. In school, they learned of the victorious battles of the partisan units and the history of the Serbian ruling monarchy. Generations grew up in [former] Southern Hungary, and their national history sank into forgetfulness.

As it was not taught in school, in some families little children heard from their parents of the heroes who fought on the Italian front, of grandfathers and great-grandfathers who shed their blood for freedom. It was that way with us, too. My grandmother told us many fascinating stories, most of which I did not understand at the time, although every word reverberates in me now like a sort-of sermon. She spoke of Count Károly Ágost Leiningen-Westerburg, who was a martyr from Törökbecse, one of the Arad 13, a major-general in the 1848–49 Freedom Uprising, who, in spite of being German-born, defended the birthplace of his wife, Erzsébet Sissányi, and fought for freedom. She told me the story of my great-great-grandfather, who returned from the Italian front during the First World War with a bullet wound, that became infected years later and eventually led to his death. I heard of the suffering of my great-grandparents in the newly formed Kingdom of Serbia, Croatia, and Slovenia, and of how, for a Hungarian, life was not good here in the Banat. And how the former Banat was sliced into three (Serb, Hungarian, and Romanian), thus ruining its economy, and how more taxes were levied on the entire region, so that the underdeveloped south of Serbia could be brought up to the level of the former — always well-off — Hungarian area of Vojvodina. This memory and situation has remained to this day in the everyday lives of people, as I constantly hear from the elderly how "They are again taking our money and harvest to feed Serbia and Kosovo."

Trianon made us far stronger, more cohesive, even richer in culture and traditions. We now value more of what we have long fought for, as a minority in our own land, and strive to regain those rights that are rightfully ours. Parents are now consciously and deliberately sending their children to learn folk dances, so that they will learn their ancestors' legacy, first through games, and later through folk culture. Thus, young people travelled the Hungarian-populated regions with their instructors, while forming personal contacts and passing on the histories of their village, family, and community, reaching the goal of having their culture stay alive for the next generations.

Tibor Bálint

A computer scientist from Törökbecse [Novi Bečej, Serbia], Bálint is dedicated to nurturing Hungarian folk culture. In spite of his youth, he has travelled to many places and has become familiar with many diverse cultures. He considers himself an accepting person. Currently, he is commuting between Szeged and his village; every weekend his heart draws him home. His days are filled with computers, musical instruments, drawing, reading, working around the house, and his university studies. He is also active in folk dancing, songs, and art, as he feels it is important to nurture and pass on Hungarian cultural values. The Rákóczi Foundation's Students Without Boundaries program, which he attended in 2016, gave him the experience of a lifetime and a number of close friends. Through this program, he became familiar with the story of Suti [a Holocaust survivor]. This left such a deep impression in him that, in his middle-school years, he prepared two Holocaust-themed programs, both dedicated to Suti's memory. The programs were presented at the Novi Sad Genius Student Contest and the Subotica Tantárgyháló, where the jury was astounded by Suti's life.

PAST AND PRESENT IN THE FOOTHILLS OF THE CARPATHIANS

Tibor Gyöngyössy

OVER the past century in what is today Transcarpathia, the accepted state of affairs has been continuous change of power and political instability. Initially, the region was a part of the Austro-Hungarian Empire, then, after the First World War, Czechoslovakia took over the reins. In 1939, it was again under the control of Hungary. After this, it became the westernmost county of the Soviet Union, called Zakarpattia oblast [Trans-Carpathia]. Since August 1991, this region has become part of an independent Ukraine. History has created a community that cannot count on who is in power at the moment, but has always tried to live through whatever was threatening it. Anyone who has visited here knows of the famous hospitality of the locals, of their struggles and their faith in God. It is the norm here to speak several languages, often in marriage ceremonies and funerals. Those living here also accept others living here. The entire population of Transcarpathia has suffered over the past century, regardless of nationality.

> The road to a common Europe ... begins with not looking down on others if they speak another language but trying to understand each other, to accept each other, whatever language we may speak.

Unfortunately, we have gone from majority to minority status in history. Many Hungarian headstones in the cemeteries proclaim those bygone days. Unfortunately, there are more and more new Hungarian grave markers, while Hungarian is heard less and less on the street. The elderly die, and the young either assimilate or move abroad in the hope of a better life. Often, I ponder whether I should go as well. Yet there are still things that tie me to this place. I have hopes that we can create a country where people live in harmony, helping each other. Over the past century, we have survived the forced displacement of Hungarians from Czechoslovakia and Malenkij Robota(the deportation of slave labour to the Soviet Union following the end of the Second World War). In Ukraine, the economic crisis and revolution caused further upheaval, along with restrictive language laws and censure which, in many cases, limited our rights. We also experienced being a Ukrainian in Hungary, and a Hungarian in Ukraine, thus forming the concept of a Hungarian in Kárpátalja. There's no point dwelling on it. Of course, we cannot forget all the retributions our innocent people suffered in the region. Alas, history — or the regime and people in power — is capable of ugly things.

Since events have turned out like this, we must try to make the best of it to be accepted as Hungarians in Ukrainian circles. It is a given that we must learn one or more languages to be able to make friends with members of other nations and prove to them that we are not so backward that we cannot talk to them. Perhaps that will alter their image of us, and it may also change the stereotype we have formed of them.

Recently, the Ukrainian government enacted a specific language law, which has seriously curtailed the use of minority languages. According to many official statements, it will help the country's minority to get ahead in the country. Many minority representatives, however, disagree, and claim this will lead to faster assimilation. Perhaps both parties are right, but it is a fact that, to attain success, you must learn the country's language. Unfortunately, this is not feasible in an environment where a child has contact only with Hungarian speakers. Instead of forcibly teaching a language, the educational system should be altered so that everyone can experience favourable conditions in a multinational country.

The country where I live would like to join the European Union. The road to a common Europe begins with cleaning up around our own house. It begins with not looking down on others if they speak another language but trying to understand each other, to accept each other, whatever language we may speak.

I remember the good relationships my grandparents cultivated with their Ukrainian and Rusyn neighbours. In fact, I have Slovak and Rusyn ancestors who also overcame the same challenges. I know what it is like to be able to talk to a Ukrainian-speaking student at university or be able to accomplish something in Ukrainian at my place of work. History has happened, we cannot change it, but the future is ahead of us, a future we may still influence, if we can show our fellow countrymen that we are open to dialogue and that we are only human. In the same way, we can ask for help from each other, the same way we can talk to the 'other,' independent of nationality, religion, or political view. We were born in the same place, and so we must retain the region's multicultural tapestry and must respect our common history. We are human beings who must learn to live in peace with each other.

Tibor Gyöngyössy

Tibor is a geologist from Ungvár [Uzghorod, Ukraine]. He was accepted in 2015 into the geography course at the II. Ferenc Rákóczi Hungarian College of Transcarpathia, obtaining his certificate as a geography teacher in 2019. Currently, he is studying for his Masters degree in geology. Tibor is an active member of several local organizations, including the Transcarpathian Hungarian Large Families Association and the Kölcsey Ferenc Technical School Self-Governing Council. As well, he is currently working with children in the Advanced Talent Development and Consultation Centre and teaches Hungarian to Ukrainians. He spends his free time reading, writing, and bicycling. He feels it is important to spend meaningful time with friends and to learn English.

THE VALUE OF OUR TRADITIONS

Virág Júlia Iszlai

IT is difficult to make an outsider understand that, although I live in Romania, I am not Romanian. I am a Hungarian, but not from Hungary. One nation, one flag, one faith, one country. Or not? The peace treaty that sealed our fate managed to create more confrontation than peace. The document was signed in a château in the Domain of Versailles, the Grand Trianon. In it, Hungary's borders slid across the map like a limp thread. Let the reader imagine a lump of polenta. In olden days, our grandmothers used to slice it with thread and distribute the pieces to the grandchildren. In the villages, they still do. The dismemberment of Hungary was similar to the cutting up of polenta. What would have happened if events had turned out otherwise?

> We agonize, oh so very much, over the past, but it is time to recognize the treasures of the present.

In my opinion, we had to experience that sense of being torn apart to fight for each other. It is a fact that man values a treasure more once it is not in his possession. Our culture became richer, our vocabulary expanded, as did our storehouse of experiences and knowledge of human nature. I could go on, but everyone's value system is unique. What would happen if we were now robbed of those? We agonize, oh so very much, over the past, but it is time to recognize the treasures of the present.

"Because a country with one language and one custom is weak and frail." (King Saint Stephen)

It was exactly one century ago that King Saint Stephen's thousand-year-old Christian country was smashed apart at Trianon. Hungary was torn apart, our nation scattered. The law regarding dual citizenship offers some possibility, on some level, to allow Magyars living in the Carpathian Basin — but outside the country's border — and elsewhere in the world, to connect with one another. The one million signatures successfully gathered in defence of the rights of Hungarians living across the border proved that we could count on each other and that we are able to come together (Minority Safepack Initiative, 2018).

We have history, a past, and a present — and we will have a future, of that I am sure. However, another question arises: Is it worth it for me to fight for something that is only half mine? With the divisions, I must unequivocally share my country with one or two other nations. A person can get into a number of problems while blindly searching for the tiny faults in one other. That is what leads to shameful outbreaks of anger at events, to insulting or laughable comments, and to various other frictions between nationalities. But those who seek will find fault in everybody, be they friend or foe, another nation, or even a brother. I must, therefore, learn that what counts is not what I think of another, or what he supposes of me. We possess a long history and admirable traditions. All these reinforce us in our Hungarian awareness, national identity, and a sense of love of country, as well as giving us a firm, secure sense of belonging. Visible or invisible threads bind us together wherever we are swept by Trianon or other tribulations.

"Do not forget, even for one minute, that every Hungarian, wherever they may live, is a relative." (Albert Wass).

The seal cannot be broken, nor the agreement voided, but we must use the opportunities as best as we possibly can. We can view events as a defeat, a victory, or a challenge. The decision is ours. It is much easier to complain, but once we experience the magical feeling of perseverance and zeal, we will want to experience it more deeply and share it with others. That is what national unity means; threads lying on a map cannot put a limit to that unity.

Júlia Virág Iszlai

Júlia currently lives in Bodos [Bodo] in Kovászna county [Judet Covasna, Romania, where she is attending high school, majoring in theology and philosophy. She is a patrol leader in the local Scout troop, volunteers in the Christian Youth Association, and is a member of the school choir and student council. In October 2019, she raised funds for the school sports clubs in the Fuss Neki! (Go for it!) event. Students Without Boundaries meant a lot to her, in that she experienced the value of minorities coming together. Among her long-term plans, after finishing high school, is university. Her interests extend to the Hungarian language, foreign languages, geography, folk art, communication, and sports. She is dedicated to learning foreign languages and plans to get her English certificate before starting university. In the summertime, she works, saving money for her long-held dream to be able to travel around Europe.

"TORN AWAY" FROM A TRANSCARPATHIAN PERSPECTIVE

Júlia Kovács

I was born in Tiszaásvány [Тисаашвань, Ukraine]. It is a typical, Hungarian-populated Transcarpathian village with its own everyday events, problems and miseries. Its first written mention in a document is from 1000 AD, when the settlement is called Asuan, and was under the suzerainty of the Kingdom of Hungary until 1920. The village was ceded to Czechoslovakia under the terms of the Treaty of Saint Germain, signed September 10, 1919, but was actually transferred following the Treaty of Trianon. After eighteen years in Czechoslovakia, the village reverted to Hungary, if only for a short period, until 1944. Then, it was transferred to the Ukrainian Soviet Socialist Republic, becoming part of Transcarpathia. Its name at the time was Mineralne. After 1991, it was a part of independent Ukraine. After a decision by the regional council, the name was reinstated to Tiszaásvány.

So, the facts are that this village, which has belonged to Hungary for 92 percent of its history, is now a part of the Ukraine and anybody who was born here, or will be, must face that fact. I have often pondered, while bicycling along the levee of the Tisza River, how different our lives would have been if, at the time, the finger of the engineer drawing the new border quivered just a bit and he drew the line two to three centimetres further over. After all, this border is only of barbed wire, not any real distance; it is not about another nation that lives here, another culture. How strange that the village of Zsurk is a few hundred metres away and I can hear the ice-cream truck go down the street, I can hear the bells calling for Mass, and hear if they announce something over the loudspeakers, yet it is in a completely different country. But I cannot go there, except with a passport. Although the same river flows beside each village, people from Zsurk can fish in the Tisza River, but we can only go on the levee with permission.

As a result of a so-called "plebiscite" held on November 26, 1944, the reallocated Transcarpathia was annexed to the Soviet Union. For half a century, Transcarpathia was a taboo topic in Hungarian politics. After 1945, it was not acknowledged; even mention of it was forbidden. The ceded "territory" had a population then of two hundred thousand Hungarians who managed to retain their identity in spite of political pressures and other prohibitive actions. There was a bit of good fortune in the calamity. In 1953, the first Hungarian-language high schools were allowed to open, although the only continuing educational opportunities for years were the teachers' colleges in Huszt [Hus] and Munkács [Mukačevo]. In spite of that, Transcarpathia enriched the world with well-known writers such as Magda Füzesi, Borbála Szalay, Károly D. Balla, Vilmos Kovács, Erzsébet Illár, and Magdolna Gulácsy.

In 1963, the National University in Ungvár [Uzghorod] started a fine-arts program and the training of Hungarian language and literature teachers was begun. Civil organizations established the Foundation for a Transcarpathian Hungarian College in 1993, since the conditions had to be created for the minorities to receive higher education. Since then, Beregszász [Beregovo] has grown into a student town. From all over Transcarpathia, in fact from outside the county and abroad, students are being accepted. The college plays a huge role in the fact that the Hungarian minority still exists in Transcarpathia, since the students learn not only the compulsory subjects but are also taught a love for their heritage, nurturing our traditions and a respect for our history.

The future of the Hungarians in Kárpátalja, or Transcarpathia, depends on whether we can retain our language, our customs, and our traditions, and if there will be anyone to whom we can pass them on. And that will only be possible if we are able to study, from kindergarten all the way to post-secondary school, in our own language. One hundred years have passed since the signing of the Trianon treaty. We can only imagine the pain of those people who lived through it in 1920. Although a lot of time has passed, while generations and political authorities have changed in this region, however, the connection of the Hungarians to their cultural ties has not diminished for a minute.

The despondency following the signing of the treaty was followed by hope, the hope that Kárpátalja would once again be Hungarian territory. With the passage of years, the hope changed to resignation. In the Ukraine we are Hungarians, in Hungary, Ukrainians, but here in Transcarpathia, miraculously, where several nations live together, we learned to live side by side, accepting our cultural differences and gliding over linguistic difficulties.

I see as the key to our survival that together, arm-in-arm, we support each other and strengthen the national awareness, maintain the schools, and create organizations that are able to draw and retain people. Programs aimed at education, the free practise of religion, and boosting the economy must all strive to make the people stay here, to find their own prosperity here.

From the events of Trianon, we have learned that what impacts our lives may change from one minute to the next, independent of us. But we also learned that, no matter how small-minded a law may be that aims to end Hungarian-language education, to erase our identity, if we stand up for ourselves and think as one, we can never lose what our great-grandfathers suffered for so long to achieve.

Júlia Kovács

Júlia was born in the village of Tiszaásvány. Even during her elementary-school years, between 2005 and 2014, she was interested in the sciences, especially mathematics. In 2014, she was accepted into the II. Ferenc Rákóczi Hungarian College of Transcarpathia, where she studied applied mathematics and tourism. She is a member of the Rákóczi Family Circle and assisted in the running of the Students Without Boundaries program as a leader. In her free time, she and her high-school friends have formed a band, *Néha banda* (Sometimes Band), In which she plays music. Among her important goals is to learn languages. She wants to improve her English, and, as a Hungarian in Transcarpathia, she wants to learn Ukrainian and Russian. She intends to get certified in the two languages. In her future work, she would like to give something of positive value to people, to humanity.

NATIONAL IDENTITY IS BOUNDLESS

Vivien Marti

JUNE 4, 1920 — a day of grief for a nation. Millions of people became stateless and woke up as citizens of another country. The redrawn border paralyzed industry, the majority of agricultural lands became foreign owned, families were torn apart.

I can proudly say that after a hundred years, years filled with struggles and desperate battles, with at times seemingly superhuman labours behind us, we are still here. We Hungarians are here in Transylvania, Vojvodina, southern Slovakia, and we are here, at home in Transcarpathia. We struggle for our language, to be able to use our mother tongue freely, to employ teachers to teach our children in Hungarian, to allow them to become familiar with Hungarian poetry and learn the history of our people. We struggle to be able to live freely in our culture, so that Hungarian folk songs and music may ring out and reveal the rich tapestry of Hungarian folk dances. We struggle for our historical monuments, so that Hungarian signs may be posted marking our thousand-year-old castles, that the Turul [mythological bird of prey] may soar freely — if only symbolically — and that the memorial to the conquest in 1000 AD does not become the target of continuous vandalism while standing as the sad testament to its own history. We struggle for the Hungarian culinary arts, to show and taste what the real stuffed cabbage of Bereg is like, to demonstrate that Hungarians make an amazing goulash. We struggle against discrimination, to be treated as equals in the workplace, and at university. Basically, we struggle for our fundamental human rights. We struggle mostly for our future, so that subsequent generations will be able to live in a Carpathian Basin where they will no longer have to struggle to maintain their language and culture.

What else could be the goal of our earthly existence but to create a better world? But what could be the key to the continued existence, development, and prosperity of Hungarians living in the partitioned territories? First of all, we must retain our faith, because that is the promise of the future. As well, there is a need for ethical rejuvenation, that people with such values as family, honour, honesty, patriotism, a moral code, and culture, again take their rightful place in society. We stand in need of an increase in numbers. The demographic data of the past decades is not favourable toward Hungarians — childbirths are declining, while emigration and assimilation are rising. There is a need to retain and pass on our language, for assurance of quality education in the mother tongue. There is need for Hungarian day care, where teachers sing in Hungarian above the crib, and a need for Hungarian kindergartens, and an even greater need for Hungarian-language schools. Our survival is the retention of our language and traditions and keeping our colourful culture alive, nurturing it, as well as coming together in the interest of a common goal. Collective paradigm change is an indispensable condition if we are to reach our goals, and the right of self-determination, which would be ensured by a wide-ranging autonomy. It must be made clear that the indigenous ethnic Hungarian minority has a fundamental right to self-determination within the successor states, as we were born there and want to live a full life, where our ancestors have lived, worked, and fought for home and country, while retaining our national identity.

Transcarpathia or Sub-Carpathia in Ukraine can rightly be called the stepchild of history. Those living there have never been blessed with an overabundance of physical possessions; this region has always been treated as a borderland, a desolate place, even if, occasionally, bright minds appeared. The serial regime changes of the twentieth century disturbed the calm of those living here. Instead of a better, more lasting, and more civilized world, it more often offered an agonizing and degrading setting for a continued existence that tried men and women. Hope and faith must be re-implanted in the hearts of our Hungarian brethren. What is impossible for one perhaps may be doable if we work together. But for that, everyone must accept the struggle. Hungary must continue to strive to develop close and friendly relations with all the surrounding countries. At the same time, Hungarian foreign policy must make it a condition of co-operation, in bilateral contacts or in international affairs, to support the autonomy and aspirations of all the territories annexed from what was formerly Hungary.

In addition to all that, we Hungarians who live in minority status must believe. We must continue to believe that, with unity, every goal is attainable. We must dream! And dream big, and fight for our dreams. We must trust! Trust in God and our fellow man. We must act! We must do everything possible to ensure a better future for Hungarians in the Carpathian Basin. We must demonstrate! Demonstrate that there are no "Hungarians from the other side of the border"; there are Hungarians in the Carpathian Basin, and these borders define the borders of our countries, but not our identity. When I was a child, I often asked my grandfather, "Why don't we live in Hungary if we are Hungarians?" His frequent reply is chiselled in my heart: "Because, when they drew the border at Trianon, the tip of the pencil was too thick." I grew up four kilometres from the Hungarian border, a Hungarian in a foreign country, and perhaps that is all it depended on: the pencil had a tip that was too thick.

Vivien Marti

Vivien was born in Transcarpathia [Kárpátalja], barely four kilometres from the Hungarian border. From childhood, her parents and teachers have reinforced in her the importance of a Hungarian identity. She is an active and constructive member of the community. During her university years, she was a member, later vice-president, of the Hungarian Students' and Young Researchers' Association of Transcarpathia. After finishing university, she received a scholarship that permitted her to live in a sparsely settled Hungarian village, Léva [Levice, Slovakia], where her work contributed to strengthening the local Hungarian organizations. She spent three years in Léva. In 2011, she took part in the Students Without Boundaries program, which made a great impression on her. She believes, "There are no Hungarians outside the borders; there are Hungarians in the Carpathian Basin."

OUR LIFE

Hanna Peresztegi

At the age of ten, all I knew of Trianon was that it was an event that redrew the borders of Hungary. I felt the effects in only three places: Slovakia, when we went for knödel [boiled dumplings] and met Hungarian people; in a camp, where a girl with an interesting Hungarian accent told me she was from Serbia; and in geography class, where we were taught about the partitioned cities, but with little detail. Take Pozsony [Bratislava] as an example. We learned that it was Slovakia's capital. The teacher then left it up to us what we did with that information, whether our knowledge would be enlarged in history class by being told that Pozsony was once a Hungarian city or if our literature teacher would be creative enough to assign an essay entitled "What could Pozsony feel?" I was very interested in finding out how it felt. Was it glad to become a capital? Was it perhaps jealous of Budapest, but would now happily take everything back to become a Hungarian city again? What must it feel like to live in historical Hungarian cities or towns like Kolozsvár [Cluj Napoca, Romania], Nagyszalonta [Salonta], or Érmindszent [Mecenţiu], which now are not geographically part of Hungary? Our teachers left all that up to us. They taught only what was necessary: Pozsony is Slovakia's capital. Imre Ady, one of Hungary's most famous poets, was born in Érmindszent. Trianon happened in 1920. Important date, remember it, it will be on the exam. This was all they added. No human perspective, no metaphors, and no personifications, and no pondering about what it must be like to be a Hungarian "beyond Hungary's borders."

We became resigned. I think that is the best expression. Resigned to visiting the house where King Mathias was born when we crossed a

> In reality, it must be terribly difficult to be a Hungarian living outside the borders.

border. Resigned that Kékes Mountain was now Hungary's highest peak. We accepted that, of the quartet of rivers on the national coat of arms, the Duna, the Tisza, and the Dráva-Száva, only two now flow within the borders of Hungary; two are gone. We also accepted that, of the three "hills" on the national crest, two — the Tátra [Tatra] and the Fátra [Veľká Fatra] — ended up across the border, both in Slovakia. They had no say in the matter whether to stay or go. The same way as the Dráva, or Kolozsvár, or the Száva, or Pozsony were not consulted in the matter. For lack of anything better, they also accepted. The Száva, resigned to its fate, trickles quietly in Slovenia, across Croatia and Serbia. The Tátra still towers proudly over Slovakia, and Kolozsvár does not seem put out to have a line drawn in front of it. They all feel that anybody who still wants to reach them will do so.

In reality, it must be terribly difficult to be a Hungarian living outside the borders. When travelling in Romania, pride took hold of me not only when I saw a statue of our great king but also when I saw living heroes and was able to talk with them. Say what you will, but somebody who does not give up and says, "Damn it all, I am a Hungarian!" then that man/woman is a hero. It matters not that he/she went to school, took exams, and worked in another language, that his/her neighbours and store clerks spoke another language. They pulled themselves up proudly and stated that they are Hungarian. At home they speak in their mother tongue, in their free time they read Hungarian, eat Hungarian foods, teach Hungarian folk songs to their children, dance Hungarian folk dances, and their hearts beat faster when a Hungarian flag flies above them.

I am sorry that most people my age only learn about Trianon only by the end of the history semester (if then). They do not delve into the human aspect of it. I ponder on this frequently. As I imagine Trianon, I have the feeling that, suddenly, I am living in a foreign country ... without having moved. How was it for a newborn, a child of Hungarian parents, to have to grown up in another country, in another language, another culture? What was it like for an elementary-school child, who had finally mastered the Hungarian ABCs and been able to draw the map of the country, when someone comes along and says, "You must learn this new language," and gives you a new map, and says, "You now live here?" What must it have felt like for a high-school student suddenly to have to take the matriculation exam in a different language? What must it have felt like to be an adult and to act as if everything was all right in front of the children, when everyone was uncertain and afraid? How about the elderly, when a huge question mark was dropped into their usual, quiet lives?

And this is just one fact in a geography class, one date in a history class, and one novelty in a literature class. Yet this is the life of others. No! This is the life of Hungarians. This is our life.

Hanna Peresztegi

Sixteen-year-old Hanna imagines her future in the world of filmmaking. Currently, she is a Grade 10 student in the Szent László Upper School in Kőbánya. From the age of seven, she has been writing stories and poems that were later adapted into short stories and longer pieces. At twelve, she became interested in photography, and has since made some short films. Hanna wants to work in filmmaking, possibly as a director or editor. In her artistic endeavours, it is clear that her Hungarian-ness is of utmost importance. At the age of ten, she expressed her feelings regarding Trianon by creating an animated short film. In her free time, she plays the piano and is learning Japanese.

A NATION OF SURVIVORS

Tamás R. Benedek

UNDOUBTEDLY, many are familiar with the history of the old man who became the citizen of five countries during his lifetime. He was born in the Austro-Hungarian Empire, lived for eighteen years in Czechoslovakia, then four years in the Kingdom of Hungary. He lived most of his life in the Soviet Union, and finally ended his life in Ukraine. The sad fact of the story is that, in reality, the old man never set foot outside the famous Hungarian city of Munkács [Mukačevo, Ukraine]. This Hungarian was not a world traveller, and was never asked if he wanted to live in other countries. He did not move anywhere; the borders were changed over his head.

Hungarians are superb survivors. During their history, they had to fight often for their country, to retain their identity, to be able to remain Hungarians. This nation was stricken by the Mongol invasion, 150 years of Turkish occupation, lethal pandemics ... and still, here we are. We live in this beautiful region and, to this day, we form the majority of nationalities in the Carpathian Basin. Perhaps we can look for the reasons behind the unjust Trianon decision in these historical tribulations, in the serious losses that afflicted the country and its population.

On this topic, I have tried many times to think like those decision-makers, searching for the reasons why Hungary was condemned collectively as being responsible for the war, as a criminal. The Austro-Hungarian monarchy was seemingly not a viable system of government. The monarchy was dissolved; it was unthinkable to have a state in Europe lording over a multinational country. Instead of one Austria, they created a Czechoslovakia made up of Czechs, Moravians, Slovaks, Poles, Hungarians, Germans, and Rusyns. They created a Romania made up of Romanians, Hungarians, Germans, Serbs, Bulgarians, Turks, Tartars, and Roma. They formed a Yugoslavia made up of

Serbs, Bosnians, Croatians, Slovenes, Turks, Montenegrins, Vends, Romanians, Albanians, Hungarians, and Italians. In fact, instead of one Austria, they created four.

In my opinion, this unjust and unsustainable dictated treaty did not create peace in east-central Europe, but rather forced the region's countries into a new world war. We know the outcome. Due to the dire living conditions and the changing world, those who could do so emigrated, and those who stayed suffered their fate. It is clear to see from the perspective of a century that foreign powers tried numerous methods to eradicate the Hungarian population or to assimilate them into foreign countries. Today, we know — and can see — that this failed. We were, are, and will be Hungarians in the Carpathian Basin. There was, is, and will be Hungarian spoken in the Carpathian homeland. After a hundred years, we can see that we are dwindling. Perhaps that is Trianon's most important lesson, that we must learn to retain our national identity, our national culture, and our Hungarian language. We must learn to remain Hungarian.

Even though the Trianon dictated peace treaty contained clear provisions that the rights of minorities be guaranteed, that has been consistently ignored by the successor states to this day.

I will never forget one favourite and heart-warming episode from my childhood, when my parents and I first visited Hungary. Crossing the border, I made a strange discovery, which I mentioned to my parents. Everything was so different. I could read everything that was written everywhere. I could not understand what changed. My father tried to explain, saying that we had come home. As a child, I could not grasp why I was taught the Ukrainian language and literature in school. I was at a loss as to where to put this strange language that we did not use in the family or anywhere else. Perhaps it was also these childhood memories that played a part in my continuing my education in Hungary, where I can learn in my mother tongue, and use it freely. That is the goal that we must reach: to make it possible for the minorities across the border to use their mother tongue and retain their culture and national identity.

The key to our continued existence is retaining our mother tongue. The only guarantee of Hungarian continuity is education in the Hungarian language. We know that, in Transcarpathia at the moment, the newly enacted language-and-education law endangers that outcome, as it restricts the use of minority languages and makes the Ukrainian language mandatory in schools. A similar law was legislated in Slovakia to limit the language rights of Hungarians. In addition, efforts are being made in Romania to gradually oppress the Hungarian minority. Even though the Trianon dictated treaty contained clear provisions that the rights of minorities be guaranteed, that has been consistently ignored by the successor states to this day.

The national politics of the current government in Hungary represent a huge improvement in the lives of Hungarians living outside the Hungarian border. Hungarian citizenship has been returned to us, a status that for many does not merely mean restitution, but gives us the sense of belonging in this enormous world. We are a part of the Hungarian nation.

Tamás R. Benedek

Tamás is enrolled in the Masters program at the University of Debrecen, studying Construction Engineering. As a result of the global pandemic, the university switched to online education, allowing him to move back to his village and follow the seminars from home. His goal, with the knowledge and education he has gained, is to move back to Nagydobrony [Velyka Dobron, Ukraine] and make best use of his education there. Tamás has unforgettable memories of the Students Without Boundaries program, which he attended in 2015. He gladly relates stories of the program to friends and acquaintances, telling them of the tremendous number of memories and the lifelong friends he obtained through the program. Each year, he encourages the young people in his circle of friends to apply to attend the camp.

THIS IS MY HOME

Norbert Bence

TIME rolls obstacles into a person's life, difficult ones that are not of the everyday kind. We all face ordeals, but what trials confront Hungarians living outside the border? What travails must they overcome living in minority status, while a member of the mother country, yet live their lives "abroad"? Can we even value what our forebears left to us in these past one hundred years?

I proudly profess that I was born a Hungarian on this tiny plot of earth. I have always been aware that it would not be easy to spend my youth in the way my heart dictated, but I will stay true to my principles, my mother tongue, and my nation.

It hurts to see the multitude of young people from Transcarpathia forced to move abroad in the hopes of a better life. It hurts to live through the separation from those I grew up with, who were part of my childhood, but are also seeking their prosperity far from home. Those who do not choose to continue their education after high school have two options: accept that they must serve in the army or go abroad to work. Neither is good. They cannot stay home because, at age eighteen, the draft notice comes. and then they are unable to build a future here if they can't find a well-paying job. Nonetheless, although many are afraid to return for those reasons, there is something that draws them home — family, friends, the homeland — Kárpátalja [Transcarpathia].

As I recall the favourite and comforting quotation from Áron Tamási, which serves as a signpost for all honest individuals in this difficult situation: "We are in this world so that we will be at home in it somewhere." As Tamási's protagonist returned from America to the tiny village where he was born, Csíkcsicsó [Ciceu, Romania], so Transcarpathian young people, adults, and old people are coming home, grasping every opportunity they can. This homesickness is proof of their love for their homeland. We can remain in the land of our birth only if we do something about it. We can try the western lifestyle — in fact, we must — but, in time, we must realize that only at home can we live according to our guidelines and succeed according to our hopes — because *abroad we are foreigners*. We can live our entire life chasing better opportunities, but nothing will bring back those lost moments that only come while surrounded by our loved ones and friends.

I was born, I went to a Hungarian kindergarten, I attended high school in Hungarian, so there was no question that I wanted to go to university here [in Transcarpathia]. In the summer of 2013, before the start of university, I went to Hungary for the third time (visits were frequent, at the time, as the border was easier to cross), and that is how I became a part of the greatest adventure of my life in the Students Without Boundaries program, organized for the twenty-third time by the Rákóczi Foundation of Canada. I lived through life-changing experiences and made lifelong friends with whom I still maintain contact.

> **They can intimidate the local Hungarian leaders, they can beat me, laugh at me, and shame me, but there is one thing nobody can do – take away my mother tongue and heritage.**

I already knew then that I would only feel really at home in Transcarpathia. After finishing my basic studies at the National University in Ungvár [Uzghorod], I was elected as president of the Transcarpathian Hungarian Students' and Researchers' Union, and I continued my education toward a Master's degree. Just before I was to receive my acceptance letter to my doctoral program, I experienced the shock many others have felt at eighteen — a draft notice came in the mail. I was expecting this, so I knew that, if my entrance exam for my doctorate was unsuccessful, I would have to go "underground" or abroad. I submitted an application — and was accepted — into the Sándor Petőfi scholarship program. I served in the widely dispersed communities of Ürményháza [Jermenovci, Serbia] and Versec [Vršac, Serbia] in southern Banat. My time spent there proved the importance of staying in our own community and carrying forward all that our forebears left to us, be it folk dances and songs, agriculture, or other family enterprises. It is certain that we will only have a future on the sliver of land where we live if we do not forget our past and carry it forward with respect, preserving what our ancestors created and left for us.

I am twenty-four years old, and, and as a first-year doctoral student, I can honestly say that we have to fight our battles. The government of Ukraine can introduce a prohibitive education and a language law, ultra-nationalists can take down and burn our national symbols, they can remove the Turul monument from Munkács Castle, they can damage the Verecke Pass marker and the Sándor Petőfi statue in Ungvár, they can intimidate the local Hungarian leaders, they can beat me, laugh at me, and shame me, but there is one thing nobody can do — take away my mother tongue and heritage. That I will never give up. It is this belief that I think is the key to the lasting endurance of the Hungarians of Transcarpathia. That is my path, which always takes me home — home to Transcarpathia.

Norbert Bence

Norbert was born in Bátyú [Bat'ovo] in Transcarpathia, Ukraine. He is presently enrolled in the Physics and Astronomy doctoral program at the University of Ungvár [Uzhhorod, Ukraine]. In 2013, he participated in the Students Without Boundaries program and believes it had an enormous impact on opening up his horizons regarding the future. Norbert is active in founding local community organizations and desires to continue to live and work in Transcarpathia.

THE ROLE OF FAITH

Réka Baricz

SINCE the Trianon peace treaty, we Hungarians living in Transylvania have often been in situations where our love of our country and faith saved us from wickedness. God has sent people and things to make our lives more bearable, easier. As well, we were reminded of who we are and what our common aim is, something we can only achieve in a united way.

We were sent a man filled with love, Bishop Áron Márton, a man who demonstrated humility and goodness all his life. The Hungarian people were always important to him. His goal throughout his life was to protect the people, their faith, and their mother tongue and traditions. He suffered a great deal during the second half of his life, but he knew that he was enduring this for his people and for the faith. As he is quoted as saying: "Don't let your faith ebb. The faith, in which we hold our salvation, the hope that has sustained us till now, the Christ-like thought for which and through which we accept our mission, will see us victorious out of the current peril as it has so many times in the past." (Áron Márton, in László Virt's *Nyitott szívvel* [*With an Open Heart*].)

I believe that our bishop wrote that for the Magyars living in difficult circumstances and in minority status. It describes our painful past and difficult present, in which we can't live in harmony, because uncertainty will not leave us in serenity. We are afraid of becoming prey to other peoples, or fear being unable to earn a living where we happen to live. At the same time, we miss the contact with our kin living far away. Bishop Márton points to trust in a provident God who will help us. We should not allow fear and discouragement to direct our lives. We must take matters in hand so that our worthy nation does not fall into the dustbin of history, we must work and live with determination and love, with faith and hope. Our survival depends on us, on how well we can think and live as one. Can we think of each other as truly brothers?

The road is long and hard, but our Heavenly Father is with us, as is the patron of the Magyars, the Blessed Virgin Mary, who helps our people and gives us faith in our everyday lives, so that we can overcome the many difficulties we encounter. Our nation has always been invigorated by our faith and shall continue to place reliance on it. If we do not have sufficient faith, then the miracle — for which our nation has been waiting for so long — will not come.

Trianon taught us to feel — to feel for our nation, to feel the pain, when we think of the peace treaty that tore a nation apart. This is the pain that all Hungarians carry to this day. It did, however, teach us solidarity, to stick together, always to think of each other as true brothers. No matter how many borders are created to divide us, we are one. We will show the world at large that Hungarians, who have endured so much suffering, are able to stand up. Even if the Hungarian people are scattered, they are together in spirit, planning the future as one, with faith.

Réka Baricz

Réka lives in Gyergyóalfalu [Joseni, Romania] in Hargita County [Judetul Harghita]. This sixteen-year-old Transylvanian is currently attending high school, studying mathematics and computers. In her free time, she likes to play the piano and guitar, read, be active in sports, draw, and stay in contact with her friends. Besides her schoolwork, she is also an active community organizer, a volunteer in the Alfalvi Kiló Kövek organization, where she organizes religious events. During the summer, she participates in Catholic camps. She has not yet decided what she wants to do, but likes mathematics very much and is planning her future in a realistic way. She sees her future in Transylvania, and would not like to leave the country of her birth.

TRANSCARPATHIA: THE CENTRE OF MY HEART

Genovéva Svingola

A hundred years have passed, a long, long time. Yet we "received something," something that beats as strong after a century as it did back then. What this dictated peace brought with it I can only comment on from a Transcarpathian perspective, as it affects all of us differently, some for the better, some for the worse. Our Hungarian-ness and the tasks that lie ahead, however, are the same.

Ukraine is attempting to modernize and would like to become a member of the European Union. However, in theory and practice, this seems at odds with the facts. Laws are passed that make the life of minorities living in the country impossible. Fundamental rights are being taken away. The use of our language is forbidden in school, at work, in offices — even on the street. The heads of surrounding countries say that these repressive laws are not allowed and can't be done by anyone, and, since we count, we have the same rights as anyone else … and yet it is being done.

> Truthfully, it is what made us who we are today: able to endure all, tolerate all, and become resilient, survivors.

We have no alternative; we would like to adapt, but how? Teachers do not receive adequate training, and there are not enough Ukrainian-language textbooks. The resources necessary to accomplish what we are asked to do are not ensured. The other big problem is that there are few jobs in Transcarpathia, and there are often occasions in which people are not hired because they speak Hungarian, even though they speak fluent Ukrainian as well. In many official situations, they simply ignore us, not taking us seriously. On the dates of Hungarian historical commemorations, they invented Ukrainian ones, and force us to celebrate those in the schools and kindergartens. They try to oppress us, whereas all we want is to live in peace and as Hungarians in our dear Kárpátalja, which is the centre of our heart, our home, our everything. We are discriminated against both here and in Hungary. They do not like us in one place because we are Hungarians, in the other because we live in Ukraine. And yet, when someone asks me if I like living in Kárpátalja, my unequivocal answer is "Yes." This is my home, everything and everyone I love are here, and I would never leave them. Right now, I am studying in Debrecen, but after university I will go home to work, as there is so much to do. Someone has to stay home and look after the Hungarians. I can see a future in Transcarpathia, a future worth fighting for.

I have often pondered on what would have happened if … I do not know. None of us can know. Perhaps much better, perhaps much worse. It is possible that we might have been discontented in affluence, but now are contented with a little. Of course, we are also immeasurably unhappy. There is a sore point in all our hearts, a wound that is sometimes torn open daily and poked at, one that will never heal. But we have learned to live with it. In fact, truthfully, it is what made us who we are today: able to endure all, tolerate all, and become resilient survivors. All the while we are alive, sensitive, and able to grasp the moment. We smile or cry at the same line of a song, we can be very joyful and can love deeply. We see the miracles of life, both small and large, because we see the world differently. We have learned to value what is ours, that tiny bit of land given to us. We sweat blood for it every day, but it is ours. Our land, our language, our culture, our songs, and our dances. Our Hungarian-ness. Nobody can take that away from us! We are in God's hands, we Hungarians. And the Creator seems particularly attentive to those of us who are separated. No matter what tribulations we faced, in all things, He protected us from our enemies.

This is the greatest strength that maintains us. No matter the number of governments, politicians, enemies, or trials that may come, we will endure. We will stay here and we will endure because we are Hungarians!

Genovéva Svingola

Genovéva is studying community planning in the faculty of arts at the University of Debrecen. As a young person from Transcarpathia, she felt it was important for her to continue her education in her mother tongue. Like many of her contemporaries, she envisions her future to be in Transcarpathia, where she wants her knowledge to lend support to the Hungarian community. Her future goal is to work for the Pro Cultura Subcarpathica civil organization, the aim of which is to nourish Hungarian culture with its programs. She attended the Rákóczi Foundation's Students Without Boundaries program in 2017, where she made friendships for a lifetime.

PART TWO

Searching for a Way
on the Periphery

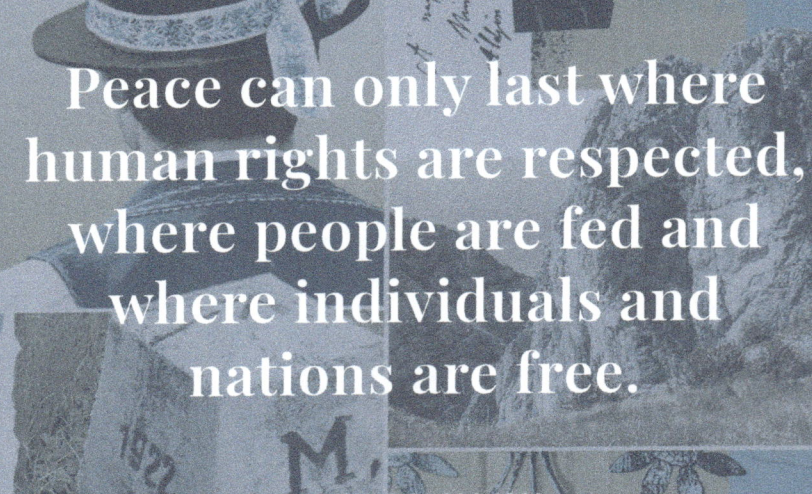

> Peace can only last where human rights are respected, where people are fed and where individuals and nations are free.
>
> — 14TH DALAI LAMA

HISTORICAL MUSINGS

Johanna Baróthi

What do the sad historical facts say?

Trianon — The charnel house of Hungarian future, where they signed an agreement so painful for millions, the harshest and most unjust punishment, the dismemberment of our country.

Trianon, June 4, 1920 — On that fateful day, all the church bells rang, factory sirens wailed, traffic stopped for minutes, schools were closed, flags flew at half mast, and the hearts of eight million Hungarians filled with grief.

What do I know of Trianon?

That if political interests require it, the end always justifies the means, and the strong think they can do anything because the weak have to bow down, must bear all.

That I have a land of my birth, a country of my birth, a mother country, dual citizenship, yet no real freedom, because Romania, although a constitutional "nation state," in reality employs discriminative treatment. It is a multinational country denying that fact, and here "at home" I am "obligated" to speak, understand, and communicate in Romanian — like it or not.

That it is an uplifting feeling hearing pure Hungarian speech when, stepping across the border, I meet my relatives, friends, and co-workers.

That tears gather in my eighty-year-old grandmother's eyes when she thinks of our ancestors, of her father, whom she didn't even know because he was a "proud Hungarian" and went among the first to fight to defend dear Szeklerland, and that, beside the map of the Szekler counties hangs a map of Greater Hungary, which reminds us that we have a right to remember that at the events of our "mournful" celebrations, when we meet a few times a year at our memorial monuments in the centre of the guild town to remember heroes, then we feel truly Hungarian under the red-white-green and Szekler flags.

That I can thank my parents' diligent upbringing for this feeling: I was born a Hungarian, and I am a Hungarian.

That Hungarians are dwindling, Hungarian consciousness is weakening, and that there is a need for the European Union to recognize the territorial and cultural self-determination of Hungarians outside the borders, so that we may become stronger.

That evoking the events of Trianon, sharing our thoughts, asking the appropriate questions, and communicating may take us closer to finding answers, solutions.

What is the condition of preservation?

A people, a fraction of a people, a minority, a community, a person, all have, as a weapon the word, their mother tongue that distinguishes their nation from other nations. The key to our preservation and continuation is our shared language, because if one doesn't know Hungarian, or doesn't understand Hungarian words, you are not Hungarian.

What is the common European future, what are the possibilities, what can we do?

The common European future is a vision, a fantasy of the creation of a well-functioning and developing empire. We know that the goal of the common European future is integration, the acceptance of those norms, values, and ideas that bind Europeans together over national and state boundaries. Sameness and a common identity or the highlighting of differences? That has long been a topic of argument among the "thinkers" of Europe. Our grandfathers and grandmothers held, as we hold too, that there is no serenity, inner calm, or happiness without knowing who you are, where you came from, where you belong, and in what direction you are going. As there is no tree without roots, there is no nation without a past; we cannot unfurl our wings to fly into the future if we lack a warm, soft nest. The civil associations here locally and in the mother country, or even those supported by Hungarians living abroad, have a large task in this. A grateful thanks goes to the

Rákóczi Foundation. For us, Szekler Hungarians living in Transylvania, the message of Trianon is clear: although power might win, no unjust treaty can rend asunder the thousand-year unity of Hungarians.

How to proceed on the path of the future?

We ask for so little and, at the same time, for so much: rights for us, an indigenous, ethnic minority, so that we can feel ourselves as Hungarians, here on the ancestral land, that we can openly cultivate our ethnic consciousness and pass it on to our children, in other words *the universal right for autonomy along with complete cultural and territorial autonomy*.

I believe it is wise to *remain a true Hungarian, to emotionally identify with the ancient Hungarian value system and symbols*. I believe there is always hope for a better future. I believe that these aims are possible, and must be acted on so that, for the youth of today, Trianon is not only a history lesson at school, to which they feel no emotional connection, but is rather a link to understanding the connections between past, present, and future — and perhaps to the wisdom we need to create a better home.

Johanna Baróthi

As a music teacher from Kovászna County [Judetul Covasna, Romania], Johanna has been interested in the world of music and the arts since her childhood. As the regional head of the Mathias Corvinus Collegium in Sepsiszentgyörgy [Sfântu Gheorghe, Romania], she works with talented young people. A defining moment in her life occurred in 2012, when she took part in the Students Without Boundaries program. It was there that she was able to realize that, despite the minority status of her community, a great deal could be done to ensure its survival in the world.

THOUGHTS ON HAPPINESS FROM THE SOUTH

Natália Gulyás Oldal

History is a series of events that we do not always remember fondly. Our country was split asunder and our lands were taken away, as were our children and treasures. Many generations worked tirelessly for those treasures, ignoring fatigue, and yet rebuilt again and again. The main driving force of renewal, the continuation of life, is a sense of unity. Together, helping and encouraging each other, we can accomplish more, much more. "Living in the shadow of Trianon, let us forget every personal affront, partisanship and offer a brotherly hand to everyone who is, in their heart and intention, still a Hungarian, even if our views differ in many things." (Albert Wass, Hungarian writer from Transylvania).

Perhaps we cannot even imagine that our little world, so tiny compared to the universe, could offer so many treasures. So many magical experiences await us during our lifetime, yet at every small obstacle we stop and weigh the possibility of retreat. It would be easier to give up, to sit at home and ignore the challenges, which would lead to an average, humdrum existence. But, having been given an opportunity at our birth, why would we not tackle it? Why would we not accomplish above-average things? I think there is the possibility for everyone to make something new, something monumental. Unfortunately, many think "That is not for me" or "I cannot do that." Not many will fight for their goals as tenaciously as they say they will. For those that do, success is not always guaranteed. But one thing is certain: the effort expended always bears fruit.

Certainly, many have pondered on what being at "home" really means. The short answer, in a word, is "everything." The long answer is "much more." I took my first steps in Vojvodina, and still live here.

This is the land of my birth and will always remain that. Here is where I imagine my future. I would like to create that "home" for my future children and hope that they will love it as much as I do.

To me, our home is where our roots bind us. It could be our village where we were born, made more meaningful by the family house, or a person who means the world to us. We must never forget where we started from, where we are going, and what our goals are. But we must not chase those goals fanatically. Only to the extent that we do not forget what an unexpected smile from a stranger means, or a long Friday evening, a strong coffee on Monday morning, our favourite music at full volume, a rainbow after a storm. We must surround ourselves with people whose presence fills us with solace and peace, not agitation and distress.

For us to be happy and well-balanced, we must also know what it is to be morose, to have fallen, and to despair. One thing we must never forget is that there is a ray of light at the end of the tunnel. It is tiny, barely visible to the eye. Yet, as we grow stronger, it does too. When in a strange city, thousands of kilometres from home, we hear a Hungarian word, suddenly mental images appear: our childhood, parents, former playmates, life back home. A warm feeling fills our heart; this is what gives us life: the search for happiness. Unfortunately, many do not realize they found it long ago.

Natália Gulyás Oldal

Natália is currently in her final year in the Bosa Milićević School of Economics in Subotica, Serbia. In the future, she would like to continue her studies in Subotica at the local Economics faculty. Thanks to her excellent marks, there is a good possibility that she will obtain a state scholarship to university; she is busy preparing for the entrance exam. She is an active member of the local Hungarian community. In 2020, she joined the local chapter of the Vojvodina Youth Forum, where she can work on important matters, something she misses since the program. Besides her studies, Natália also works in Budapest as an annotator for a publisher. After getting her diploma, her goal is to be able to work in Vojvodina.

IT SEEMED TO BE ONLY A SIGNATURE, YET IT SEALED FATES

Teodóra Gyurkó

THE twentieth century was a defining time, not only in the life of the Hungarian people but also of the world. At the end of the First World War, Hungary ended up on the losing side. The opposing sides signed the Trianon dictated peace treaty on June 4, 1920 — the Entente vs. Hungary — which made "peace" official. The country lost two-thirds of its historic territory, along with several developed cities and many important historical sites from our past. In Transcarpathia, among the first I would mention is the Pass at Verecke, where our ancestors entered the Carpathian Basin. Ferenc Rákóczi II is one of the most outstanding figures of Hungarian history. On hearing that name, most Hungarians think of him with reverence and pride. He spent a long time in the counties that form my homeland. His memory is kept alive in the fortress of Munkács [Mukačevo, Ukraine], defended by his mother, Ilona Zrínyi, the last stronghold to surrender after the Rákóczi fight for independence from the Hapsburgs. We can also list the settlement of Salánk [Shalanky, today Ukraine], the site of the last National Assembly of the fight for freedom, as well as the Turul memorial in Tiszaújlak, erected in memory of the first Kuruc victory. In the period between 1703 and 1711, the fortresses of Huszt [today Hus] and Ungvár [today Uzghorod] and the towns of Mezővár [Vary] and Beregszász [today Beregovo] played important roles. In the last two places, following the example

> Working toward a world in Europe that is liveable for all, is vitally important if we are to create harmony, co-operation, and love.

of Tarpa, the kuruc of Tamás Esze unfurled the flags sent from Brezán [Berezhany], and so began the eight-year struggle for freedom.

If I think about what it feels like to accept that, from one day to the next, our ancestors did not belong to the same country, my heart aches.

The thought "What would it be like to still be part of Hungary?" often crosses my mind. It is a strange feeling to know that the land where we used to belong is now separated from us by a border, and only can be accessed with a passport.

Personally, I regard the maintenance of my Hungarian identity as an important mission. Working toward a world in Europe that is liveable for all is vitally important if we are to create harmony, co-operation, and love. It is clear that not everything will be achieved at once, but I think that, if we can have peace, then we are on the right track to co-operation among countries. In the interest of a common Europe, we must unite, independent of country or nation.

It is sad to hear that a Hungarian is taken as a Slovak, the Transylvanian as a Romanian, the southern Hungarian as a Serb, and the Transcarpathian as a Ukrainian when we think and speak the same language as those in Hungary. Perhaps the first line of "On the Road to Turkey," by László Vári Fábián, a poet from Transcarpathia, prevails in our everyday life. We are "Orphaned in both countries." Where we now live, we are not looked at as wholly part of this country. We are merely Magyars. At the same time, when travelling abroad, we are taken as Ukrainians — and sometimes in Hungary, too. We have not been able to change where we should be living to date, nor can we change it after today. I think we are not a people who give up easily, thus the most we can do is to fortify ourselves with hope and perseverance.

A lot of changes have happened in the past few years, which have resulted in the increased emigration of families. A great many have left Transcarpathia in the hope of a better life. It is a sad fact that we are getting fewer by the day, not growing in number. For years now, many Magyar students from Transcarpathia have been going to Hungarian universities. As a young high-school student I do not see anything wrong with studying in Hungary, since that will give more opportunities and greater scope in a field. Still, we also have a great need for well-trained young people. My congratulations to all who finish with high marks at a highly respected university in Hungary. I would urge them to bring that knowledge home and put it to good use here.

It might seem unjust to expect everybody to return, since our ancestors' homeland was once Hungary. But we must face the fact that Transcarpathia has a need for every person if we are all to survive.

Teodóra Gyurkó

Teodóra is in her final year of the Nagybereg [Velyki Berehy, Ukraine] Reformed Lyceum. A large part of her life revolves around singing and music. After seven years of study, she received a diploma in the flute from the Zoltán Kodály Academy of Arts. Between 2010 and 2017, she was an active member in Sárosoroszi [Orosijevo] of Hangraforgó, a group dedicated to performing, and passing on, poems sung to music. She would like to continue her studies in Beregszász [Beregovo] at the II. Ferenc Rákóczi Hungarian College of Transcarpathia in taxation and accounting. She feels it important to nurture her mother tongue, and over the past five years she has taken part in contests of presentation, grammar, and correct pronunciation. She dedicates her free time to her favourite hobbies: reading, photography, and singing.

HOW MUCH LONGER?

Evelin Kitti Hidi

"But I have never said that word. And now, I cannot even say it, only this: something aches that is not there. Sometimes you will hear of a painful miracle of life — when someone's hand or foot is cut off, for a long time they feel pains in the fingers that are no longer there. When you will hear this: Kolozsvár, and this: Transylvania, and this: Carpathians — you will know what I was thinking."

The quotation above is from a letter written by Frigyes Karinthy [Hungarian author, poet, playwright] to his young son, in which he perfectly illustrates how unsettling it can be to speak of this historical tragedy. And yet, we have to do it, to face up to it, absorb it, accept it, and live with the situation it created.

The date is June 4. It created a new trauma for our nation, which, as our anthem says, has suffered many calamities in the past. Hungarians outside the border lost their country and became, through no desire of their own, citizens of a foreign country, against which they had no means to object. To us, it meant not merely loss of territory, but often prejudiced behaviour and harm to our identity to this day. To me, an existence as such a Hungarian means that, at once, I have two countries; sometimes I am at home in both, sometimes in neither. As such, I can feel the palpable difficulties of enduring as a group every day. During my high-school years, learning the Ukrainian language presented a continuing challenge for me. It was not from sheer laziness that I did not want to learn it. It simply was not easy — perhaps exactly because I *had* to learn it. Not knowing the language created a roadblock to success, not only in my studies, but also in everyday life. We Hungarians are frequently taunted by the Ukrainians with insulting, nationalistic insults. Our historical and cultural memorials are regularly defaced. The memorial erected in the Verecke Pass [Pereval Szerednyovereckij] has been damaged several times, as have the Petőfi statues in Ungvár

[Uzghorod] and Beregszász [Beregovo], and two years ago the building of the Transcarpathian Hungarian Cultural Association was bombed.

The continued existence of Hungarians in the land of their birth is further exacerbated by difficulties arising from the economic situation. More and more in our community find jobs abroad, resulting in families being torn apart, and drifting further and further apart. As a result, the number of Hungarians continues to decline, in both the villages and the cities. Due to the Russo-Ukrainian war that started in 2014, many are forced to leave in order to escape the draft notice and the requirement to do army service. At the same time, it gives one hope that the majority of people do not leave their homeland permanently. More and more are starting enterprises with the money they made from their jobs abroad. There continue to be children in the Hungarian-language educational institutions. There are groups that continue to conserve cultural traditions: associations and groups, folk-dance ensembles, musical groups that cultivate and pass on — even enhance — our traditions and cultural treasures, contributing to the continued existence of the Hungarians.

In 2010, June 4 was decreed as National Unity Day, and so, for the past ten years we have had a day of celebration. But do we have a unified nation? Unfortunately, we have fault-lines among us. We always had. But there is no problem with differences of opinion. In fact, I think the more multi-hued the ideas and the more different the personalities in a nation, the more valuable. Of course, there must be the proviso that this varied mix, using its own means and views, serves to develop and enhance the nation. We must not make the mistake of digging political trenches of our different viewpoints and attacking our own people from those trenches. A nation must not attack one of its own. To be able to talk of a unified nation, we must act together, and not as opposing sides. Even if we are divided by borders, we have a common purpose: the growth of all Hungarians — demographically, culturally, and economically. For that to happen, Hungarians must remain in the world, for which the most important measure is learning, passing on, and enhancing the Hungarian language, and learning our history. Further, we must gain knowledge of our culture — and enhance it— and encourage others to remain in the land of our birth, our homeland.

We now have a wider concept of a homeland that is Europe. Although Ukraine is not part of the European Union — for various reasons, still very far from it — its feelers are out toward integration with the Union.

Our generation can easily, with only a personal ID card, travel to any of the member countries, getting to know our thousand-year-old culture and historical inheritance. We can take part in the popular Erasmus program, within which we can learn or volunteer in a member country, depending on where our interests lead us — making lifelong memories and friends along the way.

To me, European integration means to rise above historical grievances, of which — just think of Trianon — we have enough, and try to live peaceably alongside each other, learning from the lessons of the world wars, striving for co-operation, guiding our communities through compromises, and expressing solidarity toward each other. There are global problems that unite us, wherever in the world we live, such climate change or the current virus epidemic. We must search together for solutions, not only for us but also for future generations.

Evelin Kitti Hidi

Twenty-one-year-old Evelin grew up in Transcarpathia, in the village of Eszeny [Esen', Ukraine]. She completed her high school in the Nagybereg [Velyki Berehy] Reformed Lyceum, after which she volunteered in the Dunaalmási Református Szeretetotthon [Presbyterian Old Age Home of Dunaalmási]. After high school, she was accepted into the Faculty of Law of Eötvös Loránd University, Budapest, in political science. As part of the Erasmus program, she worked as a volunteer in the United Kingdom in a home, the House of Light, established for persons with disabilities. She would like to continue her education at the Corvinus University in regional and environmental economics. She is most interested in climate change, and would like to learn about the possible solutions that could be used to halt that phenomenon. Further, she would like to inform the world about aspects of climate change in a more deliberate manner. Another ambition is to be able to become an intern at the European Union, to gain more insight into politics. She also feels it is important to urge others to make use of their democratic rights, especially in matters that serve Hungarian interests.

THE ONE HUNDRED YEARS OF SOLITUDE OF TRIANON

Dr. Ilona Kotolácsi Mikóczy

It is morning; the family is still asleep. As I pour my coffee, I listen to the radio with one ear: "Die Regierung hat wieder neue Maßnahmen im Kampf gegen das Koronavirus ... bla bla bla..." I switch to the Hungarian station. Regulations regarding the pandemic, the number of infects dropping, the second wave coming ... Big deal, nothing new here either. I sit down to the kitchen table and look at the messages on my phone. News from home: My grandmother died!

Click ... click ... click ... click. My thoughts flit all over the place, then like a railway ... I must go home, I must go home ... I dial my mother, then my sister. Go home, go home ... I feel flushed, my breathing is rapid ... in contrast, an icy fear sweeps through my heart. I must go home ... but how? I surf the Internet, looking at the possibilities. How can I make it home for the funeral? No exceptions, the final goodbye is not a valid reason to travel.

The most memorable experience of my childhood was my grandmother telling stories. Not of princesses, not frothy fairy tales. She told stories of long-ago courtyards, pretty girls, good-looking — but fickle — young men, old men playing cards, milk wagons, and a large shawl. She told tales of the school where she learned German and French, of who is a heel and who is a reliable man. She told stories about life. That great-grandfather was put in jail for sewing Hungarian flags. Oh yeah, and for saying to the re-Slovakization activist neighbour carrying a Slovak flag that it would be better if he threw it away. She spoke of the church where her father was a choirmaster and built a replica of the cave of Lourdes, and she recounted amid laughter that he escaped and returned after being relocated. He swam across the Danube and was hidden for a long time, but eventually got noticed … well, that is how it happened Uncle Jani got a few years for his antics. Of course, they took the house, wagon, horses, and livestock. Alas, also the school. She said, Jozsko and Anyicska just moved in, into the family house. They were not bad people basically. They came from somewhere up north, she said — perhaps from Árva [Orava County] — but probably because of a guilty conscience were not able to connect with the old people. But they did call out the secret police because more of us got together for a birthday party than was advisable. The Hungarians are congregating … always suspicious.

As a child, I often thought there was no other nation on earth that was screwed over as much as we Hungarians. My conviction was first shaken by Ivanka, the Slovak girl. We have now been living abroad for about ten years, and it was kindergarten that brought us together. Our daughters were playing nicely together, in German, and they became friends; we looked at each other with suspicion for months — she with her prejudices and me with mine. Then slowly, very slowly, we started to thaw and were able to discuss the ancestors and the situation today, and to see Central Europe a bit through the other's eyes. It was useless talking to my grandmother of my new discoveries — that you must be open to the other's point of view, that you cannot put unambiguous labels on other nations. Her generation experienced the suffering first-hand, the life without rights.

The one-time high-school girl cried out in me: when will I do well? What if I stay in the dusty, small town where I was born, from which I always wanted to escape? How far can a person's dreams fly? Where are our natural boundaries? Can we forgive our forebears for having fallen in love with Paris, Vienna, the world? And what happens if we little people also want to go? Am I a traitor if I take off? It has been years since I considered it a concern that I left the place of my birth in southern Slovakia. Today, however, I recall my grandmother, and, in spite of my logical arguments, I am wracked by a guilty conscience because I was not there with her.

For years I have reassured myself, if I thought in terms of the ancient Hungarian nation's unity, that a person living in Szeged or one living in Nyíregyháza could just as easily opt to live in Budapest as they could in Csallóköz [Žitný ostrov]. There is nothing strange in it. It is natural that the intellect is drawn to the effervescence of the Hungarian capital, its cultural offerings. Yet now … the question eats at me. I went too far away, even if only as far as Budapest. I still could not run home to my grandmother's grave. It is astounding how easy it is, even today, to separate people from each other. How fragile the freedom that befell us thirty years ago, how we attached huge hopes to the fact that the icy mountains thawed, that the majority of the countries we deemed interesting were joining the Union, that, in effect, we were being offered a solution to the separation, a way to break the Hungarian curse. It soon became apparent, however, that sweeping the grievances of the past under the rug only gives the illusion of peaceful coexistence. Until the truth can be spoken out loud, there is no real freedom.

> There is no other way but the way of reconciliation … A hundred years of solitude was more than enough for us all.

In the meantime, the family is up, and the daily grind starts. With a few words, my husband, Gábor, and I conclude there is no way to get back home. Daughter Lili announces that she has to make a presentation in her online history class about Hungary. Well then, let us start here and try out how it feels to tell the truth. The task shakes up my wounded soul. The time has come for truth to be told in a history lesson. The time has come to fill in the infantry trenches. Maybe it will be this time of coronavirus that will make us Hungarians, Romanians, Serbs, Slovaks, and Ukrainians realize, en masse, how much we need each other. During the natural ebb and flow of the centuries, we have undeniably coalesced, and we cannot do anything except shelve our self-definitions, as expressed against the "other," in the storehouse of our mistakes.

There is no other way but the way of reconciliation, and it can only be paved with the truth, getting to know and accept each other's merits, points of view. A hundred years of solitude was more than enough for us all.

God be with you, my dear Grandmother!

Dr. Ilona Kotolácsi Mikóczy

Ilona is a lawyer, having received her degree from the Pázmány Péter University, specializing in human-rights issues. For many years, Ilona worked as executive director of the office of László Surján, member of the European Parliament. Ilona took part in the Students Without Boundaries program in 1995, a fact she recalls proudly. The program exerted a great influence on her life. She is a member of the board of directors of the Rákóczi Foundation. Ilona has four children and hopes to be able to move back home from Austria and be able to do something for the Hungarian minorities in the Carpathian Basin. In Austria, as the head of the Salzburg Hungarian Association, she is an active organizer of cultural events in the local diaspora community.

HUNGARIANS WITHOUT BORDERS

Attila Norbert Ferenc

THANKS to the thousand-year history of Hungary, there are to be found a lot of successes and failures. Until the 1500s, there were mainly victories. Beginning with the triumphs of Prince Árpád, through the conquests of King Saint Ladislaus, to the numerous decisive victories of Hunyadi over the Turks. But, in the following centuries, the number of our failures increased — think of the repressions by the Habsburgs, as well as the quelling of the 1848 Freedom Uprising. However, no event put its stamp on Hungary's fate like the Trianon Peace Diktat that took effect on June 4, 1920, at 16:32, and had a serious impact on the land of my birth and the fate of the Csángó Hungarians of the Gyimes [Ghimeș, Romania] valley.

Local historian Gyula Tankó Gyula has written, "Here, at the thousand-year border, Trianon is more painful than anywhere else, as we can see daily the sick haste with which some would like to erase all traces of our beautiful history." At the time of Trianon, the valley had a population around twelve thousand, and all over Transylvania, the education law strove to eliminate the religious-based schools. The age-old Catholic institutions had to resort to superhuman efforts to maintain their existence. Children had to learn in Romanian in school, and had to speak Romanian during breaks, even among themselves. In the three Gyimes settlements, Gyimesfelsőlok [Lunca de Sus], Gyimesközéplok [Lunca de Jus], and Gyimesbükk [Ghimeș-Făget], there were ten Romanian-language public schools and just one Catholic denominational Hungarian-language school, in Gyimesközéplok.

From time to time, Romanian school inspectors would show up at the Hungarian school and, based on the school's registry, would select a few children with ancient Hungarian names and take them over to the Romanian-language school. They tried to assert that these were all Hungarianized Romanians. Thus, the names Györgyicze, Hajnal, Nagy and Jánó were arbitrarily and high-handedly changed to Gheorghiță, Hăineală, Neag, and Iuon.

The Gyimes populace would not accept that. In 1934, they began an uprising against the authorities, demanding Hungarian-language education. From 1940, when northern Transylvania was returned to Hungary, the so-called "small Hungarian world" began. The problem around the language of education for the Gyimes children was solved. However, after the second world conflagration, especially beginning in 1950, problems appeared again. It was then that the Gyimes valley was reapportioned, so that Gyimesbükk, populated predominantly by Hungarians, was appended to Bákó [Bacău] county, with a Romanian majority. Around 1963, the Hungarian-language schools in the county were closed. All the struggle for education in the mother tongue had been futile. The authorities tried everything to prevent parents from sending their children to a Hungarian-language school. As well, they had to endure tremendous indignities: the Romanians called the Csángó *bozgoroz*, or "stateless." Any application they handed in was rejected if the place of birth was stated as Hungary, the Romanians saying, "Why didn't you stay there?" My grandparents knew an old Csángó man to whom it happened, and his answer was: "Oh, I stayed here where I was born. It was Hungary that left me."

In a nutshell, this exemplifies the entire Trianon trauma of the Hungarians of Transylvania. It is clear to all that we can rely only on ourselves, now and in the future. In my opinion, we can't wait on either Bucharest or Budapest. Knowledge is our most effective weapon, and so we have to continuously develop ourselves and perform better than members of the majority nation. At the same time, it is vital to keep contacts with the mother country on a personal, institutional, and/or civil organizational level. The "without borders" programs promoted by the Hungarian government, through which hundreds of high-school students attend exchange programs on both sides of the border fills that need.

Worthy of mention is the pilgrimage to Csíksomlyó [Șumuleu Ciuc] at Pentecost, which has become a gathering spot for Hungarians of the Roman Catholic faith. Another good opportunity for young people to meet and strengthen their Hungarian awareness is the Youth Gathering of Csíksomlyó, held every August. I also encourage the younger acquaintances in my area to enter competitions in Hungary. One such program is run by the Adult College of Lakitelek, which has contests open to all in the Carpathian Basin, and which assigned Trianon as last year's topic. Another is the graphic-arts contest organized by the Army and Societal Circle of Székesfehérvár, for which more than a thousand students from the Carpathian Basin create works of art. This year's announced theme was "Who flies above in machines," and the winners were announced on June 4, our Unity Day. Such events as this, and others, are needed to strengthen our Hungarian awareness.

To live by the words of Sándor Kányádi [Hungarian poet from Transylvania]: "I am not a Hungarian from beyond the border, but a borderless Hungarian." These words must remain in the hearts of all Hungarians and these words must show the way in the hectic present of the twenty-first century.

Attila Norbert Ferenc

Attila, of Székelyudvarhely [Odorheiu Secuiesc, Romania], is spending his high-school years taking intensive English-language courses in mathematics and computer science. His passion is Hungarian history; he would eventually like to become a historian after finishing school. Besides history camps, he was part of the Students Without Boundaries program in 2019. At the 2019 Székelyudvarhely TUDÁSZ General Knowledge Competition, he placed first, thanks to his familiarity with history. He has also taken part in the Lakitelek Adult College's Hungarian history competition on the theme of Trianon, where his team made it to the final round. He volunteers with GIM, the Gyimesfelsőlok [Lunca de Sus, Romania] Youth and Public Education Organization, where he helps in organizing team-building events. He is also a member of the student council of the Márton Áron High School, actively taking part in its media group and organizing programs.

ON AN UNDERTAKING

Dr. Zsuzsanna Napsugár Tóth

I grew up in a Hungarian village, as the child of the minority in southern Slovakia, and it took me a long time to learn a second language to a middle-school level. Scouting and religion provided a lot of events around the time of regime change. Those who participated in the meetings at one and the same time learned and taught how to guard and pass on traditions. Pressure was great, since everyone held that assimilation was the most urgent threat, to the point that it defined one's choice of school as well. One was told not to continue one's education in Tatra, or in the capital. Sons or daughters should, instead, go to Hungary rather than give birth to children who do not have a nice Hungarian given or family name. The new country became the mother country. Fitting in to another bureaucracy, educational policy. Being asked: where did you come from, how long are you staying? Why are you speaking Hungarian? Why don't you speak proper Hungarian? Then comes the question of the dual citizenship. Do we want it? Well, no, we do not. Then the advantages of the Hungarian ID: do we deserve it? The cost of schooling is so expensive that mothers in southern Slovakia must earn money in Austria. Hungarian-speaking grandparents, those who have lived without the Slovak language for two generations on the outer periphery of Trianon territories, become more valuable. They are the ones greeting the student grandchildren. Then there is the worry of the Slovak language law!

At the time of regime change, there was a festival almost every weekend in the western part of southern Slovakia. Feverish fights were ongoing against globalization. We went voluntarily to teach handicrafts, as the loans that were applied for were needed for food. Time diminishes; Hungarians diminish. We study/learn to help them. Thus, social capital grows. In a "foreign" country, Hungary, we learned the beauties of our "back home" culture, while we understood it is better there. Researchers are few; there are many blank areas that are left to research. We took other courses than culture and art at university: ethnography. We got into it, and seemingly wolfed down culture. Survival was followed by revival so quickly our heads spun. What is to be done with a research team abroad? Who is to go abroad with a scholarship? Well, who is active, who is ready, who already speaks three languages fluently and has started to learn Turkish, Russian, and German, inhales learning, but is reluctant, because he/she is drained. No matter, go! Gather up the suitcase, computer, photo album, tears, and happiness. Make friends in other capitals with the progressive young people of other continents. Grandmothers baking cheese biscuits … there is no time for anything anymore. A roommate waking you up: stop writing, you have to go! Doctoral entrance exam … That is how a culture scientist drifts into a bursary when taken back to part of the former Monarchy's territory. The alibi is further research; the reason is flight.

Regrettably, far distant from southern Slovakia, three hundred kilometres away in Austria, is the new home of a bilingual Hungarian child. Here, it is impossible to make a lifelong human connection. There is no guarantee that genetic heritage is pure Hungarian, straight-line family tree, or more likely intertwined and lifelike. She knows of the Trianon borders, but her heart beats faster to borderless music. And that brings calm to the arts. Survival and revival will be elated. Southern, western, central, and eastern Europe will come together in the marriage. All this will also make the "neighbours" curious. What kind of child will be born of this? Multilingual? Identity seeker? Or children who will become what they want to become? According to their parents' most fervent wish, they are cultured and humane, and are defenders of the cleanliness of the environment around them.

There are people of many degrees of education within and outside of the Carpathian Basin. They are searching for happiness, and those ethnic traditions that, for them, make life more than bearable. I show the children the existence of "native art," of how culture and the arts sprang from it long ago. The timeline is indeed long, but through them may become the present. Perhaps a folk song is known elsewhere in Europe. Maybe the motif is of Turkic origin. With the folklore group active in Austria, we travel to a Hungarian village in Slovakia and, at a wedding feast, re-teach their regional dance, the one we learned from a professional choreographer in Hungary. And so we contribute to the diversity of the Trianon area.

To me, Trianon means respecting borders, between person and person, country and country. It taught me the most important thing: that I have a place among those who can represent the values of the nation and of its minorities in the language of science and everyday life. Would my wandering have been easier if, as a time traveller, I had embarked on my lifelong wandering in Central Europe before the signing of the "peace" treaty? Perhaps our grand- and great-grandparents already knew the answer in in their life wisdom. Maybe they would have wished their descendants a different future in February of 1920, than the one they face in March of 2020.

Dr. Zsuzsanna Napsugár Tóth

Zsuzsanna has a degree in ethnography. She has spent a decade and a half working with children and adults, especially children with special educational needs. During her university years, she received numerous scholarships: study trips abroad, art bursaries, talent scout program, Campus Hungary, Go Styria, Erasmus. Currently, she is living in Graz, Austria. Through her work, she tries to pass on the cultural elements of humanity, Hungarians, and the ethnic minorities of the former Greater Hungary through the playful language of art. In her programs, she uses the language of occupations to celebrate art and applied arts, folk art, and folk games. Her favourite method of instruction is *learning by trying* and *activity shared with someone*, as with a parent or grandparent. Their influence in the development of ability, of personality, and of family life bears positive results.

LET US NEVER FORGET TO REMEMBER!

Máté Marton

No question about it, a hundred years is a terribly long time, giving opportunity for a lot of events and changes that occur continually, sometimes to our benefit, sometimes not — sometimes both good and bad at the same time. A perfect example is Europe, especially Hungary's situation in the past century.

The year 1920 was a difficult one for Europe. Two years after the tragic war, every country was busy trying to return as quickly as possible to pre-war normality, to what the war interrupted. Unfortunately, we Hungarians were in even greater trouble in these chaotic times, because, as soon as the weapons were lowered and no more shots were fired, we found ourselves on the losing side. With the stroke of a pen, our country was dismembered, our people were separated, and people from various parts of our beautiful countryside found themselves under another country's flag. This was impossible for anyone to prepare for, let alone endure. Lives were ruined, families torn apart. Futures that had been imagined and hoped for fell victim to circumstance, because someone was at the wrong place, at the wrong time, and had his country literally yanked out from underfoot. There was nothing to do but "drift," in the hope of tomorrow — which in this case meant that the next years in the unforeseeable future might bring some change, something better for the worn-down Hungarians. Many at the time trusted that the territories governed for an entire millennium were taken away as merely a temporary punishment. Unfortunately, it was a baseless hope. The long wait did not bring about restitution, nor did any other later changes move in that direction. So, years later, we are in exactly the same situation as we have been since June of 1920.

We are part of a developing era, in which the openness of the world and its accessibility have taken unprecedented steps. This brings with it many wonderful, and irresistible, opportunities — but, at the same time, new and unknown dangers for which many of us are simply not prepared. Naturally, it does not mean that the current world situation should be fundamentally altered, since this new openness continues to provide more positives for us than negatives. Currently, the question of where we come from, of what is our history, what are our traditions, or even what language we speak has taken an entirely different position in our value system. These things may entirely escape our attention in our everyday lives. We are constantly busy, having no time for anything, really, and when we do have some rare free time, we spend it mostly on what gives us pleasure, and not on those sorts of questions that should be important. In spite of that, we cannot afford to simply forget the history of our nation, or events in world history. Anything that has happened is an opportunity to learn and to draw conclusions about how to steer things differently to bring about better conditions than those in the past. And this must be not only a personal task but a common goal and duty for everyone who dreams of a better life, a more harmonious life, for themselves and all Hungarians.

We must not forget that at certain points in life we simply cannot remain indifferent. Whoever is indifferent and has no point of view, no opinion, no firm values, can never be certain where he belongs or which way he is heading. Thus, it is important to be concerned with our past — on the level of family and nation equally — and all it entails. It is often enough to reflect on how many times we delve into the pleasures afforded by Hungarian literature, or how many Hungarian-directed films we can call masterpieces, or even how many Hungarian inventions have made our lives easier. These factors should become an ingrained part of our lives, as we are often apt to forget that we are members of the same nation, on occasion even the same country. Pride in our history and values can mean that we fully appreciate and proudly accept the country where all these inventions originated, that, yes, they are from our nation.

> Anything that has happened is an opportunity to learn and to draw conclusions about how to steer things differently.

Máté Marton

Máté Marton, from Dunaszerdahely [Dunajská Streda, Slovakia], is a lover of literature. Even in his third year of high school he had clear plans regarding his continued education: the media and economics interest him most. A large part of his free time is devoted to the arts, and he reads widely, from Hungarian literature to global, from lyrical to philosophical essays in every subject. Besides reading, he exercises his creative side by writing short stories and free verse. The stage, in which he has taken an active part, also attracts him. At present, he attends improvisational theatre — as a performer. From time to time, he has dipped into photography, studying composition. His musical taste is diverse: from Hungarian alternative rock to hip-hop. Music is part of his everyday life.

ON THE MARGINS OF TRIANON

Arnold Mészáros

TRIANON was a long one hundred years ago. Nations rose out of nothing, while others disappeared into the chaotic fog of history. Years passed, another great war came along, one even more destructive, acting like oil on a not-quite-extinguished fire. With the new war, new regimes and dictators appeared that eradicated all manner of opposition, in a brutality that was so distinctive of the twentieth century. Our forebears found themselves in other countries without leaving their homes — new countries, different rules of the game, people with a different mentality. In the interest of survival and the continuance of our nation, adaptation had to be swift. New generations had to be taught to be Hungarians amidst seemingly impossible circumstances. Generation after generation had to survive and, above all else, remain human. After many generations, I was born into the annexed Vojvodina, into Yugoslavia, into a decaying country, afflicted for years with wars. With the outbreak of war in Yugoslavia and the estrangement of people came new retributions, genocides, and various outrages against humanity. And so it happened that families expelled from Croatia and Bosnia were resettled in Vojvodina. Some did settle in, but many more focused their fear and anger on the Magyar minority living here, remembering the Second World War occupation and the proclaimed "collective guilt" of Hungarians. The majority of the later generation born into these families naturally saw a scapegoat in Hungarians. The massive resettlement following the Kosovo and Albanian massacres and the Serbianization of Hungarian-populated areas were followed by increased conflicts.

> Education for our children is indispensable. We must teach them compassion, honesty — and hard work.

As a child, I learned Serbian quickly, a skill that came in handy many times. Years later, I was able to arrange official matters for friends, and these were the first instances when I was faced with the realization that language is power, that whoever does not speak the official language of a country can never live a full life in its territory. Back in high school, I already knew I wanted to remain in the land of my birth, and to help my friends. In my later years, my guiding principle, besides my studies, was to be a good example. I was able to make friends from the furthest southern parts of the country. It was then that the idea took hold in me that, in the war for our continued existence, the first battle to be won had to be the achievement of respect. That was not fought with a sword, but with knowledge, humanity, and outstanding actions. If we lose that battle, we have no future in the annexed territories — or in the mother country.

In the region where I live, examples of well-functioning youth organizations are the Vojvodina Hungarian Student Union, the Vojvodina Youth Forum, and the Vojvodina Hungarian Youth Centre. All three are in close contact with the various groups of young people. These organizations assist students in continuing their education, helping them choose a university and organizing various events for university students. Every connective event is a step toward a more assured future. In my view, programs must be developed for young people in their twenties, to help them to develop a wider circle of acquaintances, to be able to form a strong community that is able to evolve. Those in their twenties today will become the doctors, lawyers, engineers, of tomorrow — and the leaders of the future. Relationship building and the training of the young must be coordinated. Organizing, encouragement, and support must be extended across the border for co-operation, as one never knows what opportunities will arise from a friendship between Vojvodina and Transcarpathia or Transylvania and southern Slovakia. What Trianon took away, only these connections can restore. An outstanding example of building these connections is the Canadian Rákóczi Foundation's Students Without Boundaries program. Several years have passed, yet we still keep contact with old friends [in the program] and, as long as I live, I will be grateful for the opportunity to get to know so many amazing Hungarian young people.

All of us will endure injustices and that is why it is important for us to hang on, to learn our language and history. Education for our children is indispensable. We must teach them compassion, honesty — and hard work. The more children there are who later grow into adults who display a good example and stand at the head of their community as a beacon, urging others to put aside their slights and help the nations living beside us, the better it will be. That will provide a stronger base on which we can build the continued existence of our communities. A strong establishment can only be built on a strong foundation. As our ancestors did long ago, when they built their ring of protective castles, stone by stone, in defence of their nation, so we must fight for our honour and respect, person by person, so that when we are attacked and abused as a nation, there will not be one, but ten, who stand with us, confirming our rights. With a united nation, well-regarded and with strong allies, the calamity may have been avoidable. With outstanding people and world-acclaimed accomplishments, the damage campaign carried out against us might have been deflected.

Finally, when in the land of our birth, wherever in the world it might be, we light a candle on the graves of our ancestors, let us remember that we are not alone ... and let every candle symbolize one of the hundred years on the coffin of Trianon.

Arnold Mészáros

Arnold was born in 1996 in Zenta [Senta, Serbia], Vojvodina, then a part of Yugoslavia. He grew up in Temerin, Serbia, where he lives today. In 2015, he began his studies as an electrical engineer at the Novi Sad University — in Serbian. His future thesis is the design and implementation of a modern, embedded system. After finishing his graduate studies, he wishes to get a Master's degree. His long-range goal is to start his own business to help his fellow Hungarians who do not speak Serbian to find jobs. Although his parents live abroad, he wants to remain in Vojvodina and start a family. He took part in the Students Without Boundaries program in 2013. It widened his horizons, and left him with indelible positive memories.

LET US BE AN EXAMPLE OF UNITY

Izabella Nagy

I have been fortunate that, throughout my life, I have never been embroiled in a serious conflict because of my being Hungarian, not in school, not in the community, certainly not in the family, since all around me were Hungarian families and kids like me. Truth to tell, I rarely observe such conflicts in our neighbourhood. Of course, it is all a matter of perspective and people. More often, the people having a problem with Hungarians in Transcarpathia are those who do not know history, do not know to which country this region belonged to for a thousand years or are indifferent to another's values, nationality, opinions, or honour. Personally, I cannot understand the way Ukraine is handling its Hungarians and other minorities. It is doing to them the same things as were done to Ukrainians over the centuries. It is sad that it does not respect the national values of others. Ukraine should be supporting its minorities, not quashing them. It should be setting an example by strengthening the sense of nationalism in all the minority communities, striving to erase those linguistic barriers that drive a wedge today between the Hungarian and Ukrainian populations.

> We have become a scapegoat ... if only because we do not want to relinquish our hard-won rights of education and the ability to use our mother tongue.

Although Ukraine did not exist at the signing of the Trianon Peace Diktat, in 1945, the land of my birth, then called Sub-Carpathia was annexed to it. The numbers of Hungarians living here is dwindling rapidly. The main reason is the hopelessness of the economic situation. For years, families have been relocating to Hungary. Those who remain behind must deal with the sad day-to-day experience of living in minority. We have become a scapegoat, the enemy in the eyes of the majority, if only because we do not want to relinquish our hard-won rights of education and the ability to use our mother tongue. Count Albert Apponyi, the head of the Hungarian delegation to the Paris treaty, said at the time that the successor states would eventually completely ignore the interests of those territories they annexed from Hungary. Unfortunately, the self-determination of nations remained a daydream, as those Hungarians living in blocks along the border were never asked if they wanted to belong to a new country. With the exception of Sopron and a few surrounding villages, no plebiscites were held. Hungary could not accept the new borders, thus territorial revision was the only possible path between the two wars. That produced a situation that eventually led to Hungary being embroiled in the Second World War, bringing a multitude of new horrors to Hungarians.

I would be happy if the image of Hungarians improved in Ukraine. For that, however, the co-operation of the Ukrainian government is necessary. It must realize that we have not been on this soil for well over a thousand years to take anything away from them. We did not settle into an independent Ukraine, but rather the border shifted above us without us having a choice, without our being asked. They must see that we are not their enemy. A Hungarian-Ukrainian rapprochement is of key importance if we want to remain as Hungarians here at the foot of the Carpathians.

Obviously, the retention of a Hungarian minority is crucial, not only here in Transcarpathia, but equally in southern Slovakia, Burgenland, Vojvodina, and Transylvania. The same events playing out here can be seen there as well. The census held in 2011 in most of the successor states reflects that the numbers of Hungarians in the Carpathian Basin has declined by several hundred thousand.

I believe that there is still a future for us, and for the next generations of Hungarians. But it is not immaterial what kind of future it will be. That is why we must look ahead and act now to avoid disappointment, because by then it will be too late. And, if trouble comes, it is not seemly to hide from it. Trianon and the altered borders will perhaps never be what they used to be, yet it is important for the Hungarian nation to be able to remain where it has been for centuries past, where it was born.

I would be extremely glad when a time would come when all men and women would be equal and accepted, no matter where they live and/or their cultural connections.

Izabella Nagy

Izabella lives in Csepe [Chepa, Ukraine], in Transcarpathia. Currently, she attends school at the Sztojka Sándor Greek Catholic Lyceum of Karácsfalva [Karachyn, Ukraine], where the language of instruction is Hungarian, as opposed to the high school of Csepe. In her free time, Izabella is busy as a member of the village basketball club, but she also likes to sing, dance, and participate in school plays. After finishing high school, she would like to continue her education at the Pázmány Péter Catholic University's Law and Political Science faculty. She chose that university as she feels an affinity for political science, and she would be closer to her parents who work abroad. She would like to know much more about the world, and, in this, the university would be a good guide.

THOUGHTS ON A COLLECTIVE EUROPEAN FUTURE

Nóémi Tatár Jakab

IF I had started to write this treatise a few days ago, perhaps I would have used a more positive tone. Of course, part of the reality is that, due to the pandemic raging today, we are more gloomy than usual, since we can't see its end or what after-effects it will leave behind, both health-wise and economically.

Empty nationalism will not help us to survive. It is far more important that we have well-founded knowledge and consciousness of our national identity.

Our ancestors must have faced a similarly uncertain situation a hundred years ago with Trianon. Everything they knew for certain disappeared in a flash, and they had to face an uncertainty that must have shocked them. A long time passed before we were able to process these events. In our region, Transylvania, the work of Károly Kós played an important role, urging many to choose dynamic action instead of passive acceptance. This multi-talented polymath, Kós, became an example for another reason: he was the chief caretaker of the Transylvanian Reformed Diocese, and, as such, erected a great number of churches and rectories. He approached the rift after Trianon not with words but with real action, with constructive work to try and ease the tribulations of the newly emerged minority.

The value system and world view of Kós continued to form my personality, sometimes in the background, subconsciously, at other times bubbling to the surface, but always exerting an impact. I think that the key to our survival is this: to know our history. At the same time, for our lives to be meaningful, our knowledge, values, actions, and way of life must reflect this. Empty nationalism will not help us to survive. It is far more important that we have well-founded knowledge and consciousness of our national identity — that we are aware of our stories, our history. Of key importance is upbringing — the bundle we bring from home — in that we clearly know the boundaries: what is it that we are still willing to sacrifice on the altar of a better livelihood or where the point is at which we break and give up the struggle for our survival. But the final decision is a personal responsibility. There is no universal recipe as to how we should individually safeguard our Hungarian values. It is not a problem if someone's motivation calls them away from home — in my opinion, not even if they move abroad and accept a job in another country. As long as their roots are not forgotten, as long as their children know the culture and speak Hungarian fluently, then we can speak of a dispersed — but not lost — nation. However, this forgetting is a real and threatening danger. It is reasonable to assume that a more solid sense of identity can be maintained if one is living in a wider Hungarian community than living alone in an alien environment. For that reason, the most workable solution — for me — is that I continue to live my life in Transylvania.

The land of Károly Kós is my land. It is here where I feel my Hungarian religious identity the strongest. I certainly know that not every child is blessed with such strong roots. In fact, I was not always able to appreciate being the child of a minister, feeling a detrimental differentiation in my childhood — as if people expected more from me. As I grew up, slowly I came to realize the beauty in it. There was a certain amount of trust and respect advanced, as well as encouragement and a desire to serve. Whoever accepts this will not want to exist without it. Yes, more is expected of us. In fact, I can say that each community expects more from every Transylvanian Hungarian with a higher education. The community expects that individuals will not forget where they started from, what they achieved, and will help other individuals in the community to reach similar results.

Right now, as a personal choice, I have committed my life to constructive work as the young wife of a theologian. Tremendous responsibility falls on ministers: encouragement, solace, and guidance are expected from us. It is not an easy time for the Transylvanian Hungarians. It pains us that, even from the perspective of one hundred years, our demand for autonomy is met with general animosity. But we must soldier on. To quote the words of Károly Kós:

> I shout out the battle-cry: we must build, reorganize for the work at hand. I shout out the goal: the national autonomy of Hungarians. But I also shout out: who is a coward, who is a sluggard, who wants to bargain does not belong with us because he is our real enemy, our traitor. This I shout out and want to believe that I will not be merely a cry in the wilderness, *(Kós Károly, Kiáltó szó [Words Crying Out], Kolozsvár [Cluj-Napoca, Romania, 1921]).*

Nóémi Tatár Jakab

Noémi was born in Marosvásárhely [Tirgu Mureş, Romania], is recently married, and lives with her husband in Kolozsvár [Cluj Napoca]. She is pursuing a Masters degree in marketing strategies and politics at the Babeş-Bolyai Technical University. Since 2019, she has worked at the Romanian Hungarian Democratic Alliance (RMDSZ), in the Executive Presidium, the Economic and Administrative Board, as an economic advisor. For her, the biggest challenge in the coming years will be to find her vocational fulfillment, while she adapts to new situations and moves forward. She can hardly wait to leave Kolozsvár and, as the wife of a minister, settle in a less-busy place and begin meaningful work with her husband and start a family. Almost seven years have passed since 2014, when she attended the Students Without Boundaries program. She heard of it from her husband, who was there in 2012. She passed on her impressions of the camp in her circle of friends, and, as a result, several friends also experienced what it means to become part of this community.

WHAT IS THE KEY TO OUR SURVIVAL?

Klaudia Varga

A hundred years ago, a significant portion of Hungarians were forced to continue their existence, torn away from their mother country — and that phenomenon has not changed much in the meantime. One thing is certain, we have not disappeared. Borders separate us, and it is somewhat more difficult to remain in touch with each other, but that does not destroy the national consciousness. The fact that we do not live in a common physical unit does not mean that we are separated. The agony of the past, and its present consequences, connect us and form bridges among us.

It is interesting how many things Hungarians living outside Hungary's borders have in common. We are distant, and yet live through almost the same things every day. We grew up in the winsome, heartwarming medley of two, or more, foreign cultures. It was not only the sound of Hungarian words our ears got used to. We speak its unique vernacular as our mother tongue, but include everyday words and phrases from the official language, as well as expressions of our environment. Walking on the streets of our town, we see multilingual signs, and among those languages we do not necessarily see our mother tongue. It is not certain if we dare ask for bread in Hungarian in the bakery, or in what language we should greet our loved ones on the street to avoid negative consequences. We are discriminated against due to our nationality. Here at home, we are outsiders for being Hungarians. In Hungary, we stick out of line as Serbs, Slovaks, Romanians, or Ukrainians. We are the pieces of a puzzle that do not fit into the picture anywhere. And what is the situation with the Hungarians of Hungary? Are we so different from them only because we could not live our national affiliation unequivocally? Are the wounds of the past really all that bind us together?

In my opinion, the Hungarian language is the greatest treasure that we received from our parents. Its unique beauty, the rhythmic lilt of its words, its musicality, its many-faceted expressions, make it for me one of the wonders of the world. I am proud to be among those few in the world who are able to use this language. I think that this, in itself, is a singular link.

Heritage preservation is perhaps the most pleasant way to get absorbed in history. Folk music and folk dances link us, even if, moving from region to region, they show totally different variations. The variation is not a problem, rather it signals a unique form of national culture. That these songs and dances still enjoy such great acclaim today only shows how much demand there is for this culture, as this is what defines Hungarians as Hungarians.

> **We have atoned for the past, but the future has not yet arrived. This future we will build together, on firm foundations.**

There are huge differences in our present culture, socialization, outlook on life, and behaviour. In the same way that a folk song from Kalocsa differs from one from Mohol, the same way I, a Hungarian from Óbecse [Bečej, Serbia], Vojvodina, am not the same as my acquaintances from Pest, Győr, Pozsony, or Kolozsvár. Despite that, it is nice to be Hungarian. We are all different, yet we are bound together at a far deeper level.

We have atoned for the past, but the future has not yet arrived. This future we will build together, on firm foundations and unshakable stability. We have lived through a great number of traumas, and it is highly probable that we will have to face more in the future. Perhaps we will have to make a nation that is not within one border, but is spread all over the world. It is exactly because of the possibilities that lie in this multi-coloured-ness that we will be able to overcome every hurdle.

Klaudia Varga

The art of music is closest to Klaudia's heart. From an early age, this girl from Óbecse [Bečej, Serbia], Vojvodina, has demonstrated a love of music. She plays the violin, piano, guitar, and ukulele, as well as having taken voice lessons. She has been a part of several bands, and is still active in music. Klaudia likes to learn new things, which is why she chose the computer application designer program at the University of Szeged. In the future, she would like to find a field that demands creativity, as well as being useful to society. She took part in the Students Without Boundaries program in 2016. It was an unforgettable experience for her and greatly contributed to her strengthened identity and a development of her national consciousness.

PART THREE

We Are the Future!

> What is history?
> The echo of the past in the future; a reflection of the future on the past.
>
> — VICTOR HUGO

TRIANON 100 — PAST, PRESENT, FUTURE

Réka Antal

*J*UNE 4, 1920. This date most certainly reminds every Hungarian of a reversal of fortune, no matter their age and where they live the world. Trianon was a great fracture, the likes of which has never happened before in world history.

> The key to our continuance and tenacity lies in perseverance, in making sacrifices, in uniting, in having respect and love for one another.

That Time, or Life, or History — call it what you will — presented our nation with ordeals and posed a lesson which we have had to learn all through our lives. But we, who live in Transylvania, southern Slovakia, Transcarpathia, or Vojvodina, the Magyars who live outside the border, we are an ethnic minority in our countries. We are treated as foreigners where we should not be, as we are at home. A hundred years ago the borders changed, but our heritage is still here, our ancestors came from here, our blood, our history ties us here. For us to remain true Hungarians, occasionally we must carry out acts that demand bravery, determination, perseverance, and love.

We could ask the question, "What must be done?" "Why should it be me doing anything to assure our continued existence?" The answer is simple: because you are a Hungarian, your ancestors were also Hungarian, you are responsible for the continued existence of Magyars outside the borders, so that your children and grandchildren will proudly call themselves Hungarians — will speak, learn, and think in Hungarian.

Although Hungarian is our mother tongue, we must also learn the language of the country where we live. Unfortunately, there are people who point at us just because we are Hungarian and forcefully express their animosity toward our nation. It is because of people like that that I find it important to speak their language. Often it is to our advantage to speak a language other than our mother tongue, preferably perfectly. We get an insight into another culture, which is perhaps like ours but a bit different. If we look at it from this perspective, then maybe we can see that living beyond the border is not always a handicap.

It is vital that we know our history, the Hungarian past. It is the past from which we can learn the most, that will help us avoid problems such as Trianon. It serves as an example, not just for us but for the whole world, so that such an event will not happen again. We must never forget that lesson, as long as a Hungarian is alive on the planet, and maybe even after. However, for Hungarians to endure, for us to have a future in Europe, we must not just sit and shed tears over what happened a hundred years ago. We must strive to have Hungarians come together and, with united effort, guard our culture and mother tongue.

Hungarian culture, our traditions, and our customs, left to us by our ancestors, are very colourful. We have been charged with keeping them alive and passing them on to future generations. We truly feel in our hearts and souls that we belong together when we hear a beautiful folk song or a poem, when we sing our national anthem together or take part in a Hungarian-language Mass.

György Bessenyei [Hungarian playwright], in his writing called "Magyarság," clearly stated in 1773 that "Every nation became proficient in their own language, never a foreign one." This notion of education in one's mother tongue is relevant today and will remain so in the future. Unfortunately, parents often conclude that for their child to succeed in life, it is best not to be sent to Hungarian-language school, even if everyone in the family speaks Hungarian. They deprive the child of the opportunity to learn in the mother tongue, and often life will be more difficult for the child, who does not have a clear sense of where he or she belongs.

The key to our continuance and tenacity lies in perseverance, in making sacrifices, in uniting, in having respect and love for one another. If there is a fervour in us, the spark of wanting to act, we can achieve anything. For this spark to stay alive, we are all responsible. All of us!

Réka Antal

Réka took part in the Rákóczi Foundation's Students Without Boundaries program in 2018 as a second-year high-school student. She finished high school last year at the Selye János Gimnázium in Komárom [Komárno, Slovakia] and plans to continue her education at the Konstantin Filozófus University in Nyitra [Nitriansky] in Central European studies. As a sideline, she is actively interested in history, as well as having completed a course in newspaper reporting, giving her an opportunity to try her hand at it.

THE WINDS OF CHANGE AFTER THE STORM OF TRIANON

Orsolya Bálint

THE world is rapidly changing. Everyone is striving for comfort, for innovation, for simplicity, but I wonder when we will progress to the next chapter of Madách's *Tragedy of Man*, when it will be simpler for everyone to speak one language, when the word "culture" is found only in dusty history books or perhaps on Wikipedia? Then, of course, no form of discrimination will arise if someone has better language skills and thus gets ahead more easily. Everyone will be babbling the same, reading the same news portals, believing the same rumours, and the same politician will be wooing everyone. And then, there beside the other flags, the wind will flap a wounded, torn Hungarian flag that no peace treaty or innovation can bring down. There will burst forth the anthem from many avid throats. Yes, the Hungarian flag will be there, the one they made us take down, that they banned, that was stolen years ago. When people have no time even to hate — that is when it will return. When ideals disappear from our environment is when the lessons that Trianon taught us will prevail. The Hungarians living in minority status will not give up their language. They are the only ones in the world who will understand the sonorous words they say to each other. They belong to each other, they help each other, they are happy. They will be the ones looking up from their smart gizmos. They will take part in folk dancing, carving, embroidering. The ones who will not permit the buildings of IT companies to replace their churches; the ones willing, after so many years, to don folk costume for the confirmation.

For the revolution and freedom of thought, leaders are required who, to this day, are missing from many Hungarian minority communities. This leader could be: a soldier, leading his people; a politician, gathering signatures; a talented minister, building a cohesive community; a teacher, instructing the Hungarian students about awareness and pride. In the case of discontent and unrest, the question always comes up: "What is the point in fighting?" "How is a Hungarian better than a Romanian, or a Serb?" If they are all the same, "Wouldn't it be easier to disappear into the crowd, to sidestep the issue?" What makes somebody a Hungarian, and others non-Hungarians, is national pride. Something ties everyone to their homeland, some deep intellectual and spiritual values, while other reasons are the simplest of things. Some call me childishly optimistic, but I truly believe that Kolozsvár (Cluj-Napoca) will be Hungarian in spirit as well someday. It will be enough to fly the Hungarian flag beside the Romanian. If the Hungarian signs are left up on the streets. If the Romanian festivals accommodate the minorities and we can also freely celebrate our festivals. If I can talk on the bus in my mother tongue without it bothering anyone. The city will truly be ours when a Romanian person, of their own free will, chooses a Hungarian restaurant if the food is better there — even if they do not understand me but at least accept me, my family, my friends, my people.

I believe there is sense in staying ... because it is easy to leave, but to leave behind a cohesive, strong community is far more difficult.

I believe there is sense in staying, to rebel or accept, because it is easy to leave, but to leave behind a cohesive, strong community is far more difficult. It would be hard to leave the memories, the wild countryside, perhaps even the two-lane major highways, the bright red bicycle lanes, too. Everything happens for a reason. It cannot be accidental that we were born here, we grew up here. Our mission is here! The mission must be discovered individually, but you should never turn your back on where you live, why you were born a Hungarian here.

Orsolya Bálint

Orsolya is in her final year at the Báthory István Elméleti Lyceum in Kolozsvár [Cluj Napoca, Romania] in mathematics and information technology. From a very early age, she has been interested in Hungarian history and took part in many associated projects and monument-preservation activities. She is thinking of continuing her education, but wants to remain in Kolozsvár, where she likes living and staying close to her family and friends. In her free time, she likes to be outdoors, gladly going on hikes in the mountains and taking bicycle tours. She is pleased to volunteer in organizing and running these outings. A lot of her time is spent studying, but there is enough of it left for her to take part in economics and physics competitions, or her other passion, playing the guitar. In the future, she plans to take an active part in the community's life: organizing events, online advertising, and, further afield, perhaps volunteering or participating in archeological digs.

THE ROAD TO ACCEPTANCE

Ágnes Fekete

THE hundredth anniversary of the Trianon peace diktat … It is interesting to savour these words. The anniversary seems to be in the distant past, but measured in years, it is exactly four times more than my age. Yet those few words have turned into a perception in people's eyes. One that, as a Hungarian, we can never think of positively, even in part.

> In my Europe, all the various nationalities can … safeguard their cultures, but also exhibit curiosity about the customs of those living around them.

As one from the Partium, I feel I have not been born into the post-Trianon pain, or perhaps we did not have traumatic feelings around the event. As a result, for a long time I did not grasp what it was all about. Twenty minutes from the Hungarian border, living in a city where there have always been Hungarian television and radio programs, I did not understand for a long-time what people were lamenting. As a matter of fact, if someone mentioned "Mother country" or "Greater Hungary" in a moment of nostalgia, I got offended. This was the country of my birth, my culture was not in a foreign place, unreachable, far away, but primarily here in Nagyvárad [Oradea, Romania] where I live. Of course, I grew older and saw many things, experienced many things, and I now understand, as far as I can, what they are talking about when they talk about the injustice of the past.

Perhaps this is a utopian idea, but when the Romanian-Hungarian question pops up in a conversation, I always have the feeling that if either party (and many times this falls to the offended party) would try to go in the direction of *understanding* and *being understood* instead of *anger* perhaps, in time, the defining part of the conversation would be about the similarities and not the differences. That could perhaps lead to *acceptance*. It is easy to be angry at a lot of people for what happened. But, as I see it, it was easy for the ordinary people of that time — as it is easy today, too — to stoke aversion against a person who is your neighbour, who lives next door, and who confronts you on a daily basis, by saying that you have become a foreigner in a country your ancestors settled centuries ago. Similar disharmonious thinking is mirrored by the "new residents," who, for decades, have been fed historical lies and today rightly worry for their homes because of a conspiracy theory that Hungarians will retake the areas that were removed from Hungary many years ago. And since the fearful subject cannot be broached cautiously enough, since they cannot know which Hungarian is the one already at work on the plot, it is far easier to be wary of them, to hate them, since they are so close.

The only remedy I see for this is to get to know each other. Becoming familiar with the history, the story, and the people. My key argument is that we are responsible for our own decisions and our lives. Similarly, the other camp can only account for the lives they live. The Hungarians in Transylvania are angry at the Romanians because they had to grow up in Romania, but I think everybody should agree that the population of present-day Romania is in no way responsible for what happened one hundred years ago.

Speaking for myself, I can honestly say that I hold myself fortunate for recognizing how much knowing Romanian culture, having Romanian acquaintances and friends, has added to my character. I need not feel less of a Hungarian as a result. Rather I can say that I am Hungarian despite growing up in Romania. Putting it like that, I am filled with a bit of pride.

I do not think the key to our continued survival is to form closed communities. On the one hand, we must remember who we are, because, in our memories, in the past, is hidden the wisdom that helps us through today and nudges us toward a better future. For another thing, it is worth surmounting the pain of the past and going beyond the grief toward mutual recognition, so that we may live beside each other in peace, knowing each other's values. For me, it equates with modern European existence. In my twenty-first-century Europe, all the various nationalities can exercise their traditions and safeguard their cultures, but also exhibit curiosity about the customs of those living around them. If there is to be peace among the nations, politicians can say anything, they can try to close Hungarian schools and universities, to make education impossible — but if the people living together know each other, they will see through these situations and will take a stand beside each other.

We must waken that person in us. Over and above that, we must teach our beautiful language to our children, nurture our traditions. and teach our history. We must make an example of our humanity to them and to our companions. We must protect ourselves from attacks, but must not let self-defence be our permanent attitude. A man who feels a danger is in a restricted state of mind, unable to see clearly. Perhaps the time has come to decide how we would like to exist. For me, an existence worthy of Hungarians means to retain, even to raise us — but to elevate our fellow countrymen as well.

To me, culture, national self-awareness, and history are concepts not dependent on external factors but the feeling and knowledge I carry within me, which I take with me, wherever I go in the world.

Ágnes Fekete

Ágnes has travelled around the world as a puppeteer. She received her diploma in 2016 in Kolozsvár [Cluj Napoca, Romania] in theatre and drama. Her career began in the Griff Puppet Theatre in Zalaegerszeg, from which she moved to Veszprém in 2019. A career highlight was the 2018 performance for babies in Taiwan that she attended as a result of winning a creative competition. Among her long-term goals is to return home, to be able to demonstrate the accumulated knowledge of the past years. The Students Without Boundaries program remains a fond memory for life, from which she still retains friendships. No matter to which Hungarian-populated region she travels to, she usually meets former friends from the program. She is thankful to be part of the Rákóczi Family Circle, and that she is made to feel at home wherever she travels in the world.

MY TRIANON

Ágota Regina Hidi

THROUGHOUT my life, there was never a question about whether or not I was a Hungarian, in spite of the fact I do not live in the mother country. I grew up in a small village where they cling to traditions. I know the customs, the folk songs, the folk sayings, everything that a person my age living in Hungary would know. We are no different in this regard. Yet I have never felt that this is true, as many others haven't. We Hungarians, living outside the borders can say we have never found a home.

In the land where I was born, as in other parts of the Carpathian Basin, one can observe large-scale emigration. There are many reasons for this. One fundamental reason is livelihood — the lack of jobs, or the draft for military service that affects every young man. Another important reason is the lack of any vision about the future. We young people have many questions about what to do and where we should plan our futures. Unfortunately, we cannot change the past, but there are some ways we can direct what is before us. Because of that there are responsibilities weighing on our shoulders, since we must make decisions that will affect the rest of our lives.

Many scorn those who work abroad or, for various reasons, decide to move abroad, saying they have "betrayed their homeland," or "taken the easier road." I wonder which is the easier, more liveable, road? To stay or to go? It is a dilemma for many of us. If you stay, you will be with the family. Whatever happens, you will have someone to count on, as there are relatives, friends, and acquaintances who will stand by your sickbed or help in a difficult situation. If you decide to move to the mother country, then you will be far from everything, everyone. You will have to learn to live in a new, strange environment, but you will be certain that your child will one day certainly go to school in Hungarian, can live as a Hungarian, can feel whole. They will not have to live through all that you had to — such as being immediately laughed at in a store if you put the accent on the wrong syllable, or worrying when you go to a doctor that you will not understand what the doctor says or be able to communicate what hurts and where.

Although the memories will hurt, "parts" of you will be missing, but the future generation is more important than you. Even if people move away, they can still teach their children to respect their heritage and be proud that they are Hungarian, even living outside the border. Whichever side of the border we choose to live on, we all swell the Hungarian nation. Together, we can tend to the traditions and customs and enhance our history — not forgetting the roots — and visiting our grandparents can help us remember together.

There are those who choose to remain, trying to make their present lives more liveable. Those people attempt to retain their Hungarian-ness by speaking Hungarian to their children, sending them to a Hungarian school — as long as possible — retaining traditions within the family, and eating Hungarian foods. They live, believe, and hope as Hungarians.

Interesting that both choices have common elements: the future, children, and posterity.

Ágota Regina Hidi

Ágota is a third-year student in the history program of the II. Ferenc Rákóczi Hungarian College of Transcarpathia. A defining moment of her life came in 2017, when she participated in the Students Without Boundaries program. The camp was important for her realization of who she is and helped her experience her Hungarian-ness. She took piano lessons as a child and dances in the local folk-dance group. Thanks to her successful application to college, she was able to spend time in Budapest through the Erasmus program, which she enjoyed very much. In the near future, she wants to finish college and earn her diploma. Then, she wishes to continue at a Masters level, probably in psychology or the environment, both of which interest her.

THE KEY TO OUR SURVIVAL

Éva Andrea Kántor

WITHOUT question, Hungarians think back on the events of Trianon with aching hearts. After a hundred years, we still regard the past with sorrow and an anger that gnaws at us. We blame Fate, the series of events, but that does not move us ahead. For us to be able to maintain ourselves, we must build up the resiliency of our community, get over the grievances of the past, and be able to see the possibilities of the future.

> Trianon is, unquestionably, a part of our national identity, but we must not let it be the ruin of the nation.

The key is: building value, more precisely the recreation of values, a new definition of worth. Values today are relative. Preservation is only possible if we can pass values on, finding the means to make traditions — the concept of "home," of being a Magyar — a value for the next generations. The storehouse of opportunity is endless, so the question is, what will we find at the end of the chosen path and how will it help our preservation? That makes it crucial to develop a preservation strategy and devote adequate energy to it.

To be able to live in a secure country and be able to create a stable future, independence is necessary. Independence can take many forms. If economic autonomy is not successful, people are apt to forget that it does not preclude anyone from creating their own economic independence. Starting new enterprises can be the basis of a sort of independence, taking aim at the local markets, as well as making us financially independent of the state. Starting a new venture carries no small responsibility but, looking to the future, it opens opportunities for the younger generations to find work, to have a stable income here at home and not have to go abroad to work.

Besides ensuring financial benefits, it is crucial to safeguard cultural assets. Our world provides ample opportunity to get to know every culture on the globe. If there is no well-developed cultural medium where young people come face-to-face on a daily basis — and not just occasionally —with our traditions, then they will drift away from Hungarian culture. Traditions must not only be respected but must become an integral part of our souls, an inextinguishable part of our psyches. Often, it is not a museum visit or a history class that accomplishes this, but some pursuit in which young people can take an active part that helps in preserving culture.

An important element of cultural preservation is modernization. It may seem trivial, but a lot of the young are buying wallets, backpacks, and modern, stylish clothes with folk motifs on them. Isn't it wonderful to think that a mix of culture and modern consumer items contributes to keeping the most ancient traditions alive? Moreover, more and more festivals aimed at young people are being organized, where the aim is to acquaint them with Hungarian folk music. As well, what takes place is not simply the teaching of folk songs but the pairing of folk songs with modern music. Through that, a young person not only becomes familiar with thousand-year-old melodies, but also learns to make them personally relevant today, finding a link between the past and the present. These innovations in the fields of fashion, music — or even gastronomy — reinterpret cultural elements translating them with the eyes of today into a more understandable language. That is how culture becomes popular: by playing a huge role in preservation.

The future will not be constructed by crying, again and again, over the past. Trianon is, unquestionably, a part of our national identity, but we must not let it be the ruin of the nation. Bitterness must be replaced by an individual's desire to fight back by replacing conservative views with modern ideas that retain the old foundations but motivate the creation of something new. That will convey a message to the young: this is your culture, this is your home, this is your destiny!

I truly believe this is the key to our preservation.

Éva Andrea Kántor

Éva Andrea is a Grade 12 student at the Bolyai Farkas Elméleti Lyceum in Marosvásárhely [Tirgu Mureș, Romania]. Last summer, she was preparing for her matriculation exams, and the Trianon essay competition. Her plans for the future include studying mechanical engineering at the local Sapientia EMTE institution. During her university years, she wants to do research and development work alongside her father, who is a mechanical engineer. She took part in the Students Without Boundaries program in 2019.

QUESTIONS ON THE ETERNAL EXISTENCE OF A NATION

Réka Kelemen

It has now been one hundred years since Hungary suffered the indignity of the Trianon peace treaty. The country's territories were lost, and with it the Hungarian nation, or so the Great Powers thought. A hundred years have passed, and still the nation stands proud. The attempted annihilation failed to eradicate our people. Weakened, yes, but the Hungarians survived.

> We cannot alter the past, but the past is not behind us, it is within us.

Many dream to reverse Trianon, but would that be the best solution? Just think about it. Would our nation be stronger if we all belonged to one country? Is it necessary for every Hungarian to be on one side of a border? Today, that is questionable. Crossing borders, keeping up contacts, is not a problem today, so I do not feel it is necessary for a border to keep us together. Naturally, there would be many advantages, but it would not exert undue influence on the nation. The real question is the preservation of the nation. There is strength in numbers according to an old saying, but a nation does not become a unit based on territory. Far better to think of it in terms of mental unity — common goals, common dreams, and a common way of thinking. Today, you can be anywhere in the great wide world and, if you declare yourself to be a Hungarian, then you are a part of and a supporter of the nation. You may be inside or outside the borders, but if you accept and preserve the identity, you can contribute to your people.

Perhaps that is the most difficult part: to persevere — not only outside the borders but inside as well. Not only to exist in the country but to remain a Hungarian with a clear identity, in body and soul. The continued existence of a nation lies in cohesion. How do we pull together, we Hungarians? We all have one goal: to make the Hungarian nation live on. Although that may be the goal, it is not always apparent in our actions. Together we may commiserate over the past, over Trianon, together we may blame the great powers, and others, but can we act as one for our continued preservation — together, as a nation? We often point fingers at other nations, blaming them for our decline. The Hungarians outside the borders are, in many cases, not seen to be Hungarians. Hungarians living abroad look down on those living in the mother country, while those who moved abroad with their families are called the biggest traitors. In these cases, nowhere do we find even a shred of the concept of unity. In fact, we find the opposite: fragmentation. This discord is about who is the more Hungarian. We must forget that argument. There is no such thing as somebody being more Hungarian than somebody else, no such thing as somebody being the most outstanding Hungarian. There can only be Hungarian individuals and a Hungarian nation. We have no need to qualify Hungarians with descriptive adjectives.

True, Trianon was an injustice, but it happened a hundred years ago, and today we still grieve and mourn. The time has come to straighten up and turn our negativity of the past into a positive world view. Let us leave our meditation on the tragedy to the annual day of remembrance of Trianon and try to find the sunny side of things on the other 364 days. With positivity, unity, and co-operation we can improve the nation. A better and more beautiful future may await us if we can incorporate those three things into our lives.

Looking at all of Europe and the European Union, as we take part in the progress of the EU, an opportunity opens up for us for a freer Europe. We can be a constructive component of a community that offers numerous opportunities. One opportunity may be the creation of a more united, cohesive community of Hungarians in the Carpathian Basin, which could have positive influence on the nation. alter the past, but the past is not behind us, it is within us. If we find the right direction, then we need only take the first step and proceed without turning back or veering off.

Réka Kelemen

Réka grew up in Transylvania, in Kézdivásárhely [Tirgu Secuiesc, Romania], going to school there in a class focused on natural history. Presently, she is a first-year university student in Kolozsvár [Cluj Napoca], studying computer science at the Babeș-Bolyai University. Her next trip will take her to Holland to spend an university year as an exchange student. Among her long-term plans is obtaining work experience after finishing university, at home or abroad. But, in the end, she would like to put her knowledge to use at home and bolster the Transylvanian community with her work. For her, social life has always been important, while scouting and being active in the theatre world have always taken precedence.

WITH UNBROKEN FAITH

Árpád Konnát

AFTER Muhi [1241] and Mohács [1526], Trianon, the deepest tragedy of Hungarian history could — and does — fill volumes. Yet I think, in connection with this event, it should not be grief but hope that fills our spiritual world. If the flame in our hearts for our country dies, our love toward our close or extended community ebbs. If we can't maintain the fire of faith — primarily in God, of course, and secondarily in our temporal and spiritual leaders — if the light of reconciliation goes out in our surroundings, in our situation, then hope may still give us strength for a new start, to work toward a better future based on the past. I will now sketch what I think are the long-term means for our continued existence in the Carpathian Basin, what we can do on an individual and community level so that a hundred, a thousand years from now, Hungarian will still be spoken in the territory of historical Hungary.

> If they get to know us better, their potential antipathy toward us will decrease or ... they will be more impervious to manipulation against us.

The first — and in my opinion central — reason that led to the Treaty of Trianon was demographics. Part of it was not our fault, but part of it was. And that is something we can do something about in our present situation, and must do for long-term continuance, even in the separated regions. The creation of families, the bearing of children, is the most important factor in our continuity. Apart from demographics, an important factor in our times, as it was generally through history, is the economy. A hundred years ago, we lost the food industry, a major portion of heavy industry, as well as significant agricultural, mining, energy, and industrial capacities, and also energy sources. What solution can there be in which we ordinary persons can take part? First of all, as much as possible, we should always buy from a producer in the community, always buy local items. Our money should go into the pocket of the corner greengrocer or butcher instead of to a multinational concern. Choose the product of a small winemaker, so he can put food on the table and send his children to school. As the money circulates among us, any potential government opportunities offered for assimilation have less interest to us.

A solid tower of strength for continued Hungarian existence is education. Sándor Reményik [Hungarian poet from Transylvania] warned: "Do not forsake the church and the school!" This point links back to the first, that the key to long-term continuance is the number of children and, what is more important, their education, both at home, in school, and in the community. The most spectacular example in Transylvania goes back to the 1930s, when a map showing the results of a survey of those who were able to read precisely delineated the areas where the majority was comprised of Hungarians, Szeklers, and Saxons [Germans]. Within these ethnic groups, the proportion of the educated was far higher. This higher level of education must serve as a bastion in our time. It will also encourage the members of the current majority to send their children to Hungarian-run schools, where they may receive a greater insight into Hungarian culture than they do now. If they get to know us better, their potential antipathy toward us will decrease, or, put another way, they will be more impervious to manipulation against us. It is a lesson of the ages, from various historical periods and eras, that, by and large, it is illiterate individuals who can be easily influenced by various hate-based ideas to commit violent acts. High-level and modern education will also present us with an opportunity, on an international level, to find allies to our cause. In the matter of education, the final word — our main aim and element of our continuance strategy — must be a higher standard, as a means to spread the truth. *The truth shall make you free* [John 8:32]

But we must stand firmly on the ground, which, in practical terms, means, when possible, choose a partner from your own community, have as many children as possible, provide them with roots, and send them to Hungarian-language schools. Moreover, we should work here at home, buy local produce, hire ethnic Hungarians if we have a business, and choose Hungarian companies when looking for work. We must also continue to train ourselves, mentally and physically, to be spokespersons for the Hungarian cause and to tell the truth on the international stage. All the while, we must stand firmly on the Earth and keep our eyes on the Heavens. From there not only are our ancestors looking down at us from the Milky Way, holding our hands — on a spiritual level — while we retain and respect their memories. From on high, God also smiles on us and sends a message in the beautiful poem of Sándor Széllyes [Szekler poet, storyteller] not only that our suffering may be a little more, because we are more, but that those who withstand it will be saved.

Árpád Konnát

From the place of his birth in Transylvania, Kovászna [Covasna, Romania], Árpád was accepted to the ELTE University's Faculty of Arts in Budapest, studying history and archeology, focusing on the Age of Migration and the Middle Ages. Currently, he is working on his Masters. While in university, he acquired practical experience by taking part in excavations of prehistoric, Age of Migration and Middle Ages sites, both at home and abroad. In the summer of 2015, he was part of the IV. Russian-Hungarian archeological expedition at dig sites in Russia, organized by the Pázmány Péter Catholic University. As a fourteen-year-old, he was one of the youngest participants in the Rákóczi Foundation's Students Without Boundaries program. After finishing his studies, he hopes to move back to Transylvania.

A CONTEMPORARY NATION THAT IS SURROUNDED BY ITSELF

Erika Ködöböcz

JUNE 4, 1920, disastrously sealed the fate of the Hungarian nation. At ten o'clock in the morning, the assigned time of the signing, our nation died for a moment. A moment of silence was observed all over Hungary, church bells rang, flags were lowered to half-mast, vehicular traffic stopped for ten minutes, stores closed. Families and friends suddenly found themselves on the wrong sides of borders in a mutilated country. From the scope of a hundred years, how can we portray this period? During the past hundred years — as has happened so many times in our long history — the Hungarian nation has received innumerable wounds from world wars, as well as from internal retributions in the aftermath of uprisings and regime changes.

> Opportunities must be ensured, as we organize for dignified recognition of our celebratory occasions, for bringing to life — and sharing — our customs.

In the eyes of a person of today, any emphasis on the pains of the past has been shifted to the experiences of the present. In the centre of Europe, the task that awaits us is to prevent those hundred years from being forgotten. We must step past the last stage of the grief to be able to build a new existence for the future of the Hungarian nation.

As a former participant [of the Rákóczi Foundation's Students Without Boundaries program], I could fill reams of paper recounting my experiences, but there is one feeling that I do not need to recall, as it still lives within me today. I met a lot of young people during the program, all of whom came from the countries surrounding the mother country. We knew we represented the values of one nation, we were merely the ones under the visible surface. That feeling was and is a sense of unity, a sense of belonging. It is strengthened by a common language, in which our mothers sang to us, which fills the spaces at home, which poets use to address us across the span of a hundred years. To be able to find themselves, every child, every young person, needs to experience this sense of belonging while searching for self-identity. Creating it is not only the responsibility of parents, of a nation, but ours as well. As a Hungarian who lives in Transcarpathia, I have unfortunately seen that families are being torn apart in the hopes of better job opportunities. Mothers raising their children alone, grandchildren left in the care of grandparents, present a distorted image for the economies of the successor states. We cannot blame the families for the emigration.

We must approach the problems caused by the Trianon peace treaty with openness and culture and learning. We must put aside our pride and must prove to those now outside the borders that their discernment makes them worthy of these benefits. Presently, we can reach a large percentage of people in seconds through telecommunication, yet we barely make use of the opportunities. Lack of empathy often springs from misinformation and from a lack of information. But I feel it equally important to remember the borders of the former Greater Hungary at our national holidays, both within and outside the country.

But I wish to bring closer the feeling of unity. Let us embed that concept in our everyday lives. Many thousands of young people and adults are engaged in the activities of the many organizations outside the borders. I am on the board of the Transcarpathian Hungarian Cultural Association's Youth Organization, which is active in our town. The collective represents unity to us and serves as a link between the separated region and the mother country. By ourselves, is difficult to overcome the pain of the atrocities that befell us, but we are not alone. To be able to proudly accept our Hungarian-ness, we must first know who we are, what values we represent, and what cultural traditions we cling to. We must find our place in the micro-, meso-, and macro-system where we live.

As part of community unity, I think it important to mention the possibility of practising religion. Our country has, for a thousand years, declared itself a Christian country, and the current population identifies itself as followers of some religion. The village where I live is a few dozen kilometres from the castle of Munkács [Mukačevo, Ukraine]. In the centre of the village the Reformed church stands proudly, and it fills me with pride that latecomers to services usually find only a few empty seats. There, everyone greets me with a smile and asks about my health. Each Sunday, the people of the village find it important to celebrate unity with the word of God. Community members keep our traditions alive to this day, and the minister serves as a spiritual guide.

One of the important goals of community life is to focus on the preservation of national identity. Our national identity is defined by our history, by our communities, by our mother tongue, and by retaining and practising our traditions. But to have traditions to live by, they must not only be preserved but brought to life. That responsibility falls not only to the Hungarian-language schools, to the leaders of groups, villages and settlements, but to all the members of small communities. Opportunities must be ensured, as we organize for dignified recognition of our celebratory occasions, for bringing to life — and sharing — our customs. A nation's culture lives, and grows, through everyday events. Let us not be afraid to display the tricolour on March 15, make time amid the difficulties of everyday life to listen to the stories of our grandparents, to read a word or two from a Hungarian writer, to watch Hungarian movies, and to get to know the outstanding heroes of our Hungarian cultural history. Bring the past closer by for the entire world to enjoy by using the means of the modern world.

What we lost through Trianon cannot be restored, nor can we alter the mistakes of the past. We have been labelled as citizens of another country. Yet our mother tongue, our historical past, and our cultural heritage lives in us, and cannot be extinguished. We live with the results of the actions of strangers, yet we have a duty toward our country. Globally and individually, we have a responsibility to make sure our children's Hungarian awareness supports that country.

We must act! We must stand up and build the nation with bricks instead of tears, never forgetting those borders, those mountains, that were once ours.

Erika Ködöböcz

Erika is in her final year at the Eötvös Loránd University, studying special education for the mentally and psychologically challenged. She attended the Students Without Boundaries program in 2016, which represented a defining moment in her life. She gained a wealth of experiences and made a lot of friends. In her spare time, she plays the piano and reads. She truly loves the western poets of the twentieth century, the scent of books, and poems that she occasionally commits to paper. Her pieces of prose have appeared in newspapers and on internet portals. Her plans for the future include continued education and finding a job in her field. Her fiancée is a Protestant Reformed minister-in-training, and, after their wedding, they plan to serve together in a parish.

HOW TO PROCEED DESPITE THE COMMON PAST

Emőke László

DURING my university years, I had a teacher who, although a "good Hungarian," berated people for making too much of Trianon, but always forgot about the Second Vienna Award. As a Hungarian in Romania, you might think that I continually live in the shadows cast by these two — and other — decisions and changes, but the opposite is true. I come from a tiny town in the centre of Hargita [Harghita, Romania] county, where Hungarians and Romanians live together with one common enemy — the police — but that is fairly typical of a lot of settlements. I completed my university studies in Kolozsvár [Cluj Napoca], where, surprisingly enough, even less conflict can be found— in fact, hardly any. The people of Kolozsvár were not bothered by my broken Romanian. I think perhaps it was during the Students Without Boundaries program in 2014 when I first heard of the past that we all share. Since then, I have studied for three years in university, more than enough time to learn of a world which, in my mind, borders on a work of fantasy. I mean, how many people today fight for intangible ideas? How many are willing to give their life for "their country"? In my studies, I have come across the European ideals, the voices of minorities, the clash of cultures, and the celebration of regional differences. But one thing has never changed: our past defines us, and few would give that up for a vague, common future.

I am a believer in peaceful coexistence. We can achieve change if we merely look forward; the cultural differences are a perfect place to start a dialogue. We are all Hungarians, in Transylvania or in

> At the heart of coexistence is the freedom to celebrate everything together, share our traditions and grieve quietly.

southern Slovakia, Vojvodina, and Transcarpathia. In fact, one can hear Hungarian spoken on the streets in the most remote corners of the world. Yet we are all unique. It is tolerance that helps us live together, but we need time to learn how to develop it. Perhaps it seems utopian right now, but, with tiny steps, we may reach a stage where it does not matter where I come from, only what I have become. As a first step, I would encourage learning the languages in every country. That I, as a Hungarian, speak Romanian is an advantage, because I can understand all those living in the country who speak the "shared language" and the country's official language. To become accepted, we must accept others and open doors. Mutual interests are not bad, but they only work in a Kantian world, where people think logically, rules are obeyed, and oversight is not required.

At the heart of coexistence is the freedom to celebrate everything together, share our traditions, and grieve quietly, within the cultures, on those black-bordered days. Something communal must be given to people to hang on to, a shared identity, for them to feel at home with others. A new and necessary element to achieve a near-utopian future is time. A new generation must grow up, with a clean slate, to be able to accept a style of life offered by the future. We must get rid of — or at least push into the background — the phantom hand of the past, which chokes us before we can take the first, unsteady steps. Let us base our lives on common foundations and agree on rules we can obey and ideas that take us forward. Let us base our future on solidarity, co-operation and helping each other. Let's choose accomplished leaders who truly look toward the interests of the imagined, ideal future. Let us be brave and seek — by devoting the time necessary to understand — the other's viewpoint. Let us take small steps toward a better future that does not demand victims … for which we are unwilling to sacrifice.

Let us celebrate the cultural differences. Let us be the citizens of a global village where we would like to live. Change begins in us! Proceed with small steps, open and willing to accept.

Emőke László

Emőke is currently in her final year of a Masters program, as well as working in marketing. She plans to continue her education, to progress in her field. She is planning to write a book in her spare time. The thought came up a year after she took part in the Students Without Boundaries program in 2014, but has since become an obsession. She came across the Trianon essay competition on a social-media page and started to write down her thoughts as a mental distraction. During the writing of the essay, she realized that it was more than just a piece of writing, rather it was a dream she could be a part of — "a shared future does not spring from one notion, does not come into being overnight, the change starts within us," she wrote.

I SMILE AT THE WORLD BECAUSE OF WHO I AM!

Krisztina Magosi

WHEREIN lies the key to our persistence and continued survival? My answer is simple: within ourselves. We have to clarify who we are and what we would like out of life, from our country, and, not least, from the world. Remember the words of the very famous Hungarian poet, Sándor Petőfi, who stood and addressed our people: "Rise up, Magyar, the country calls! It's 'now or never' what fate befalls" [from the "National Song" by Sándor Petőfi]. It makes one think. If we, collectively, do nothing to ensure the future of a cohesive nation, then we must be prepared to accept that we will perish, a little at a time. We can do something for the continued existence of our nation. For others to believe in us, we must believe in ourselves. Believe that nothing is impossible for us, that we are always there for each other, no matter when or what the problem, holding hands and praying to God.

I ponder on what could happen if everyone — every beating Hungarian heart and gleaming eye — could unite and strive for a better future? Although many things come along in life to open our eyes and shine a light on what and where we went wrong, we cannot imagine the moments where the attainment of our goals is impossible. We fail to grasp a kind word, a smile, the words of a young girl, who no one hears because she is without experience, yet she has hopes for the world and her country. A child's smile, an encouraging word, a solitary teardrop.

I smile at the world for who I am. At people to make them feel that we belong. I call to them in the name of everyone, for them to see something through my eyes, to hear something a girl once held dear. A destiny, a life, a nation. A teardrop shed by the world... for the behaviour of people, the attitudes and lack of empathy, for thoughtlessness, ignorance — for itself. Yet I still believe in people, because I feel I must. I believe in a better future, because my belief is my destiny. I believe that we Hungarians would do anything for each other in trouble. I believe that our apathy will not always be so widespread.

Do not forget that if you believe in what you stand for and proudly accept the consequences, if you persist with what, for you, is crucial and, although people take no notice of you, strive to do everything in your power to effect change — the world will slowly change, by you and around you. You are the key. The future depends on you. Change depends on you, and you are the one who, with a glance or knowledge or an idea, can enrich the world, and this may have a ripple effect on the future of your nation. Trianon gave us a lesson that tested every Hungarian. Put your hand on your heart and feel your Hungarian spirit — even if you are but a drop in the ocean, life would not be complete without that drop.

Krisztina Magosi

Krisztina Magosi was born in Szabadka [Novi Sad, Serbia], Vojvodina in 2000. She lives in a small village called Orom. She attended high school in Szabadka at the Polytechnical school and finished a course to become a technician in the printing industry. Krisztina lives with her father; her mother passed away seventeen years ago. She is unemployed, and has experienced difficulty finding a job because of the Serbian language. As a hobby, she has recently started to write poems. During the pandemic, she has spent time with friends and family. Regarding the future, Krisztina will do everything possible to find a job and be able to have a financially independent life. She took part in the Students Without Boundaries program in the summer of 2018. The program provided her with experiences to last a lifetime, with many new friends and an extended family.

NURTURING OUR ROOTS

Kinga Noémi Mezey

ACCORDING to some history books, when Napoleon asked François Talleyrand the well-known question about what to do with the Hungarians, Talleyrand supposedly replied: "Sire! It is an ancient custom of the Hungarians to remember their heroes. They are proud of their past. Deprive a people of their past and you can do whatever you want with them!" Every tree can easily be destroyed by its roots, even the tallest one, and so it is with Hungarians. For that reason it is important to know our past, our roots.

One of the best ways to get to know history is not necessarily by reading books, but by listening to our parents and grandparents and hearing the real stories. There is nothing in the world like the feeling when you crouch down at your grandmother's feet and hear of a historical event — in the first-person singular — from a personal perspective. The tales of ancestors, the memory of brave warriors, the tenacious, never-halting history of Hungarians is the most beautiful story that can be passed down through generations. Our history is a gift from heaven, a treasure we must respect and safeguard. The brave deeds of our ancestors stand as proof that, even in the darkest of times, we — the nation — stayed strong, did not lose hope. Their role now is to kindle warmth in our hearts, to give us strength and will to proceed, even if countless dangers threaten.

Our history also lives on through our traditions. It is important not to forget them; in fact, we must continue to bravely cultivate them. Folk traditions are integral from the perspective of cohesion and our continuance. If a sort of spiritual bond forms with our customs, they will later increase in value — take a central role — and we can pass them on to future generations with love and appreciation. There are countless organizations that have the goal of retaining and nurturing traditions and folk customs. Personally, I am a member of the Turul-Sas Traditionalist Association and the Turul-Sas Order of Knighthood, which, among other things, keeps alive medieval traditions. The main goal is to retain for posterity our Christian, Hungarian identity, as well as the traditional Hungarian values. Becoming familiar with our history creates a stronger spiritual and intellectual bond between individuals and the nation.

A sense of national identity is strengthened by travelling through the Carpathian Basin. It is important to get to know our country by immersing ourselves in it to understand our past. I count myself among those fortunate ones who have had the wonderful, memorable opportunity to take part in some of those programs. Hungarians coming from different countries — even continents — have forged strong ties. We are seemingly connected almost spiritually — the world is ours. The strings that tie us together are invisible, but unbreakable. Distances between us have disappeared, uniting us. We radiate honest, open happiness for one reason only — because we are able to be together. We dared to be ourselves in this inhospitable world that forces us mortals toward perfection. Now we are complete for each other. My spirit soars, like the turul [mythological bird of prey] in the sunshine ... brave, proud, happy. It has bloomed like a tulip in the Hungarian fields ... joyously, playfully, with bursting heart. I will never forget visiting the tomb of Ferenc Rákóczi II. when we were in St. Elizabeth Cathedral in Kassa [Kosice, Slovakia]. Hungarian young people, strewn all over the world like crumbs, stood, as everyone bowed their heads and paid their respects to the great prince. It was here where I truly felt that, no matter where fate may take us, we belong together.

> Our common roots connect us, something no one and nothing can rip from our sacred soil, no matter how far our lives take us.

To be a Hungarian does not mean our address documents refer to the same area, between certain borders. To be a Hungarian is a mental state, a way of life. To be a Hungarian is a decision. Our common roots connect us, something no one and nothing can rip from our sacred soil, no matter how far our lives take us.

To close with the words of István Györffy: "Being a Hungarian is not a question of body, nor blood but a matter of spirit."

As long as we serve our nation faithfully, and regularly nurture our roots, the tree of Hungarians, reaching for the sky, will bloom.

Kinga Noémi Mezey

Kinga comes from the city of Nagybánya [Baia Mare, Romania] in Maramure? county. She finished high school in the local Németh László Elméleti Lyceum, focused on biology and chemistry. She was studying for her final exams at the time of writing this Trianon essay. In the future, she wants to continue studying the sciences, thus she applied to the Bábes-Bólyai University in Kolozsvár [Cluj Napoca] to their chemistry and chemical engineering faculty. In that field, she took part last year in the Candin Liteanu chemistry competition sponsored by the university. The university counted her result as a bonus point. Besides chemistry, she would also like to take the pedagogy course, as she likes to work with children and feels it important to help the next generation with her knowledge. Her hobbies include painting, drawing, and reading. In the summer of 2017, she took part in the Students Without Boundaries program. She feels it an honour to be a part of the Rákóczi family circle.

AN IDENTITY ENCODED IN THE SPIRIT

Emilia Peleskei

THE centenary of Trianon brings both sorrow and joy at the same time. We grieve over the loss, being torn apart, yet we have reason to be happy, since, despite the passing of one hundred years, we have not disappeared from the map and can look with hope to the future. Being Hungarian is a value: we know a unique language, a distinctive culture, and belong to an exclusive community. We are a worldwide community, present in the Carpathian Basin and numerous places in the world.

> Language is one of the most precious gifts that we can pass on from generation to generation. Our mother tongue is our most defining feature.

"A chief attendant of a healthy nation is a national language because, as long as it survives, the nation lives" (Count István Széchenyi, *Hitel*). Therefore, the continued existence of our Hungarian-ness lies in our mother tongue. Language is one of the most precious gifts that we can pass on from generation to generation. Our mother tongue is our most defining feature. Through it, we get to know the world and the world gets to know us. We may speak several languages, but throughout our lives there will be only one language with which we will have a close and intimate relationship: our mother tongue.

To the question of facing countless difficulties every day, I would say, "Yes, every Hungarian does." The truly difficult task is for dispersed minority communities of totally divergent backgrounds and situations to find the path that leads to the retention — and even strengthening — of their ethnic identity. After a century, Hungarians remain, and thereby Hungarian heritage also remains. Here I am thinking of the Hungarian language, culture, traditions, churches, and monuments. Retention of a heritage speaks not of the past but to the future, as our traditions and customs define us and, through them, we can take pride our heritage.

Folk customs are not only important as retainers of a culture. These events and celebrations are what unite Hungarian communities, bringing much happiness and pleasant moments. The Easter sprinkling of village girls, Christmas nativity plays and beigli baking, dressing up for Carnival, erecting a maypole, these are all Hungarian traditions that bind the nation together. It is well known that at whichever gate a maypole stands, a Hungarian girl lives within. Those distinguished days, such as the day dedicated to Hungarian poetry, to the martyrs of Arad, to the anniversary of the 1848–49 Freedom Fight, all reinforce and deepen our Hungarian identity.

Our national cuisine, cooked by our parents for us, has become a fundamental part of our cultural heritage. No wonder Hungarian gastronomy became so famous worldwide. Who does not like a goulash soup, a meat-broth soup, stuffed cabbage, and other such gastronomic specialities that impressed all at the Brussels World's Fair?

Another key that is indispensable to the continued survival of Hungarians is Christianity. We must retain it and bolster it in our own interest. Without the presence, strength, and service of the churches, the odds for the continued existence of Hungarians would be much reduced. The communities of faith accept significant service in maintaining local Hungarian communities. That is why the nurturing, appreciation, and maintenance of these institutions is so important. The Christian religion is certainly bolstered in the hearts of people if they can read the Bible and praise the Lord in their mother tongue.

Why does our continued existence depend on these factors? Because these can't be erased from people. They can't be torn away "just like that," as some would have liked to do with Hungary. As God made me a Hungarian, I feel it is my duty to keep and pass on this heritage. My birth was not accidental, nor was it an accident that I was born Hungarian. Every person is born with a purpose and, for us Hungarians, our biggest mission is to carry forward this heritage for future generations.

Because I am a proud Hungarian, and because it is good to be Hungarian.

Emilia Peleskei

Emilia spent her high-school years in the Péterfalva [Pyiterfolvo, Ukraine] Reformed Lyceum. An American teacher working there arranged for her to spend three months in the United States, where she volunteered in several places and learned English. Later she was accepted into the political science and law faculty of Debrecen University, where she is today, focusing on her studies. She participated in the Students Without Boundaries program in 2017, where she realized that "it is not only those of us in Transcarpathia who are oppressed, but all the other countries where Hungarian minorities live as a result of Trianon." She recalls that summer and the invaluable relationships she made with deep gratitude.

HOMEWORK FOR A LIFETIME

Enikő Sőreg

TWENTY-ONE years ago, my spirit moved into a body, and I came into the world. I was born in possibly the most beautiful part of the world. My home is the Great Plains, home of rivers and fertile fields. My first words were in one of the most difficult languages in the world, Hungarian. I learned poems and songs in this dear, ornate mother tongue, yet I was not brought up within the borders of Hungary.

> In the life of a young adult, the confusion of searching for an identity is ... multiplied if a person is growing up in an area where he/she is in minority status.

In the everyday life of a young adult, the confusion of searching for an identity is fundamentally present. This is multiplied if a person is growing up in an area where he/she is in minority status. In Hungary, you are called a Serb, in Serbia a Hungarian. Well then, where do I really belong? For a long time, I did not grasp what a treasure I had in my hands thanks to this mixture. I came to realize what a wonderful thing it was to represent the Hungarian nation in another country, and I would very much like to live my whole life here. It is very important to build, unite, and nurture the Hungarian community that is here. Among other things, a small community was formed a few months ago here in Zenta [Senta, Serbia], where we place such things in the forefront. The role and support of the community is extremely important for continuity. Our group researches and seeks out members of the older generation who can provide us with useful knowledge. A significant part of the continued existence of a nation is the knowledge, use, and transmission of the stories of our ancestors, thus nurturing our people's traditions and values.

Over the past hundred years, our world has been taken over by globalization, which makes it more difficult to retain our nation's heritage. Thanks to that, a good number of ancient crafts have disappeared over the years. The key to our continued existence lies in building communities. No wonder they say that there is strength in numbers. The more we deal with that, and create such a community, which guards our nation's traditions and language, the stronger we become. Perhaps one day we may reach the point where we are in the diaspora and do not feel like an outcast nation, but like an asset, and feel at home. The more people to whom we can show the treasures in our dear motherland — thinking here equally of monuments, the multitude of farmlands, and natural treasures — then perhaps fewer will emigrate and will come to realize that they have a task here, in this region — and not just any ordinary task.

Through our celebrations and events, we can gain a sense of belonging to the universal Hungarian nation at a school closing graduation, a New Year's Eve celebration or an Easter Sunday service, all of which add different meanings to our being part of a culture. The Hungarian wedding traditions of Vojvodina, communal pig-slaughter and grape-harvest festivals, are all events that can be tied to ancient customs. With the butchering of each pig, seemingly nothing goes to waste as we continue the traditional ways handed down from our ancestors. At Easter, we eat the smoked ham put away the previous winter, along with home-raised eggs. Wedding traditions now differ a bit by region. In the village of Zenta, typically it is the best man who directs the festivity. In Temerin [Temerin, Serbia], the custom is different. They say that the people of Temerin know what to do; they have no need for the best man. The csardas and the kóló [Balkan circle dance] are equally part of the festivities, which comes from the fact that we are a mixed nation. Our celebrations are closely tied to religion. Our faith provides a strong basis to our culture. During the Communist era, my mother learned a particular line of a folk song as "who knows when we'll see another." Thankfully, I learned it as "God knows when we'll see another."

I am certain that other Hungarians living outside the borders feel as if they have grown up in the wrong country, and thus see it as their fate to be outcasts and unwelcome, even though it's a hundred years since we were so cruelly torn away. With justification, some say that there is no need to be resigned to this fate, but to strive and fight not to be a part of the current country. I personally think that fighting against this situation will be like battling against windmills.

We must really get to know our roots, which now bind us here. We must not let this treasure be wasted, the treasure that our local culture represents, although it is a huge lesson to learn. By uniting, we can show the powers-that-be that, no matter how much they try to oppress us, the phoenix always rises from the ashes, each time stronger than the last. But as long as people leave the country merely for financial gain — from the intellectuals through the skilled workers to the farmers — we will have a hard time creating a strong and independent community.

I believe that while there is even one Hungarian-language cultural event, church, school, or civil organization, all is not lost, and we have something to hang onto. We must not allow these values to disappear; rather we must strengthen and build upon them.

Enikő Sőreg

Enikő was born in 1999 in Zenta [Senta, Serbia]. She finished both elementary and high school there, focusing on mathematics. Currently, she is studying applied information technology at the Technical College of Szabadka [Novi Sad]. She was a participant in the Rákóczi Foundation's twenty-second Students Without Boundaries program in 2015. She likes to spend her free time in community building, handicrafts, and working in the garden. Her immediate goal is to finish college, followed by a postgraduate Masters program — while still in Vojvodina. She can visualize her future only in Vojvodina, and would like to work there, while actively building her own community.

HEAVEN AND EARTH, SAINT AND SINNER, OR OUR TWENTIETH CENTURY, OUR TRIANON

Dr. Erzsébet Fanni Tóth

THE calendar reads 2020. A hundred years ago something was torn apart, something many called ideal, a blissful condition. On top of it, it is exactly seventy-five years since the end of what can honestly be called the earthly Hell of the twentieth century.

I grew up in Perbete [Pribeta, Slovakia] halfway between Révkomárom [Komárno] and Érsekújvár [Nové Zámky] in the 1980s and 1990s. Trianon, the Vienna decision, the Arrow Cross, the Russians and the Germans, and Horthy and Beneš were frequent topics around our table. That "the front came" was heard as frequently as "the hens are laying" or "the corn has to be hoed." The winter of 1944 and 1945 stayed with us permanently. The same with Julius and Stevie, who will always remain twenty years old, not having returned from the battle of the curve of the Don River to grow into proper old age. Then the "Czechs" and "Hungarians" too, along with Aunt Ilka and Uncle Rezső, or aunties Julcsi and Zsófi, who were moved far away by a forced deportation or a population exchange. It was a red-letter day when their puffing train brought them home — to us — from far away. You see, we were the guardians of their childhood, the aroma and flavours of home. They visited us once or twice a year, or when the political and economic situation permitted, to be replenished. For them, we were the desired roots, the past. For us, they were the desired wings, the future.

There are people whose fate is to wait: the Lizzies and Andys who learned in their childhood from the ABC textbook that "I believe in one country, I believe in one nation, I believe in the resurrection of Hungary." Then the wheel turned, and they waited for there be a school, if the war ended. That we *will* be able to meet with relatives and friends, if *one day* we somehow return from deportation. Eventually Waiting — with a capital letter — quietly seeped into all their cells and became part of their lives. Waiting for siblings, nieces, in-laws, and godchildren, now far away on the other side of the border, to again be able to sit around the family table, because then it will be good, really good …

The waiting, the yearning, becomes so ingrained in these people, becomes so much part of their everyday lives, that they no longer notice that, instead of reality, they propagate an imagined — a hoped-for — world. Until they face that reality, the storms of history, the ethnic- or religious-based discrimination, then their desired world (it was once, and may be again) will always be as they colour it. Full of love, warm hugs, prosperity, and unity.

> Let us finally step on the road to healing, so that … a hundred years after the peace treaty of Trianon, finally, without shame, remorse, and angst, this can be the inner path to our own peace.

My generation inherited the weight of yearning. The great opportunities in the years after the regime change of the 1990s permeated us, then we progressed into a wide-open world after joining the European Union. We, the grandchildren of deportees, the great-grandchildren of the population exchange, grew into a fantasy world, along with the real world. And we believed that, one day, we might go, as everyone else did in our families … to a thousand-times imagined place that unfortunately never existed and probably never will. Then, while the elderly stand at the garden gate, looking at us in the distance, waiting for grandchildren, we young live in airports, on Facebook, Netflix, and TikTok … in an equally dreamed-of, and now virtual, world, just as generations before us did. We keep saying, "If the Coronavirus ends…" or "If I get my diploma/get promoted/pay off my debts…" If … if … if.

The ability to bear, to accept, to live and co-operate with others is what contributes to the healthy growth of a person's character, and only then is one able to live a full life. And this ability to accept, to face reality (but not be crushed by it), is what is crucial if we are finally to find our place in Europe and among the people of the world. Trianon and the

Second World War and its subsequent border modifications burdens *every* Central European family, independent of nationality or religious affiliation. Decades later, it is now overpoweringly necessary to finally end the mourning and step past the received and inflicted wounds. The road to healing is nothing more than the acceptance that the past is closed.

We must see and appreciate what the present and the future can offer us. We must appreciate that we now live in a free Europe, where we can learn in our mother tongue. We in 2020 do not have to resort to ensuring our continued existence with the aid of a stamped document of exclusiveness. But it is up to all of us to ensure that this freedom will be enjoyed by future generations. We want them to enjoy the richness and pride of a dual — or even more — identity without lamenting our Hungarian heritage or questioning it. We, all of us, must take action to create a world where our children can sing in German, count in Czech, play in English, and have supper in Hungarian, if they wish. Their reality, their inheritance, can be and should be inclusivity, acceptance, and even plurality. They should not have to live through Hell while chasing visions of an elusive Hungary. They should not be called saints if they choke the multi-dimensionality in themselves and force others to do the same, and they should not be called traitors and criminals for not loving (only) in Hungarian.

Let us finally step on the road to healing, so that we can truly be what we have always been … and are. A hundred years after the peace treaty of Trianon, finally, without shame, remorse, and angst, this can be the inner path to our own peace.

Dr. Erzsébet Fanni Tóth

Erzsebet Fanni Tóth was born in Perbete [Pribeta, Slovakia]. She obtained her education at the Selye Janos High School, and later received scholarships at Utrecht University and Central European University. Dr. Toth received her doctorate in Psychology and teaches at Sigmund Freud University in Vienna. She is founder and CEO of Femspace, an organization that provides workshops and mentoring programs for Hungarian women who live in the EU and who want to continue their education and start their own businesses. She started an oral-history project for the elderly members of her home village on Facebook at Stories from Perbete (Perbetei Életmesék). She took part in the Students Without Boundaries program in 2001 and is an ardent supporter of the work of the Rákóczi Foundation. Dr. Toth has participated in many international studies and conferences and has a particular interest in migration, trans-generational trauma, and societal roles.

PART FOUR

Canadian Voices

Because a unilingual country with only one culture is weak and frail.

— KING SAINT STEPHEN

USING THE PAST TO BUILD A STRONGER FUTURE

András Z. Diósady

GROWING up in Canada as the child of immigrant parents you very quickly realize you lead a double life. For me, the first half of life began in a Hungarian world. Everyone around me spoke Hungarian, we did many things according to Hungarian customs, and the yet-unknown majority of Canadians outside my immediate circle didn't understand. The other half started to develop when I started school and didn't speak the common language, English, and the other kids had no clue what I was saying or referring to, but I was not alone in this feeling of being different.

I imagine that any member of Generation X or later, growing up in a major North American metropolis, would be intimately familiar with multiculturalism and the challenges it presents in the schoolyard. With childish innocence, we recognize people are different, but probably don't understand why. Logic would tell us that, since we were born here and raised here, we should be similar.

From my earliest years in school, I had classmates from all over the world, and they all brought a bit of their culture with them. In addition, every year there would be new arrivals, immigrant children whose parents chose to come to Canada looking for a "better life." These students wanted to fit in, and they looked to existing students as new friends to help them fit in. If I look at multiculturalism as an ideal from that age, multiculturalism in a school setting meant that everyone brought something with them: new games, new rules, new experiences, new traditions, new languages. They immediately made a positive impact, introducing new games, new methods for learning, new experiences. At other times they left us more confused, we didn't yet understand our own customs and traditions, and then here comes someone with customs and traditions that were completely different. But fundamentally, we were able to achieve what Canada has always strived to achieve with multiculturalism: a collective learning and improving of our society through collective strengths and experiences.

> Students Without Boundaries is helping the region to achieve its true potential ... developing a group of young leaders who are able to impart an inclusive, positive influence across the region.

The great thing about the freedoms of this country is that this collective experience carries over, even generations after ancestors arrived in this country. Cultural heritage is most often looked at as a positive addition, and parents encourage their children to dedicate time to their cultural heritage. This takes many forms during the formative years, including language schools on weekends, active participation in community events and programs, as well as the less formal cultural experience within the home. These of course come as a form of sacrifice, time dedicated to something we don't fully understand as students. In many households the question gets asked, "Why do I have to go to school on Saturday when my 'Canadian' friends get to watch cartoons or play outside?" Often, with age and wisdom, the advantages of having an additional language, a culture, and a community become clear, though as children it appears to be a penalty imposed by parents. It is also only with time and wisdom that we begin to value having multiple cultures.

Through many years of extensive travel and work around the globe, I realized that this ideal of multiculturalism with which I had been raised in Canada is very far from normal, though perhaps the largest lesson to be learned is that there is no world "normal." Over the years, I have experienced such a diverse set of reactions that it is hard even to summarize them. I have been everything from an odd curiosity that people gather round to stare at, to the other extreme of being a target for terrorists to attack. There has been the assumption that I have money, and that I should be taken advantage of. I have had preferential treatment based simply on my skin colour and the nationality of my passport. Regardless of the characterization, even in the worst of these scenarios, I could only consider myself extremely lucky to be a Canadian while abroad. Sadly, what I witnessed in many places was discrimination or hatred of other races or cultures, the view that others are to be taken advantage of simply because they are different. This can manifest itself as brutally as in slavery or simply as small hurdles that make everyday life more challenging. However, in any case, it is a far cry from both my Canadian values as well as my experience as a white male.

Despite all my years of exposure to minority-rights violations, it was at the Rakoczi Foundation's Students Without Boundaries program where my exposure to minority-rights violations started to mesh with a deeper understanding of the prevalence of these issues and a yearning to start addressing this on a wider scale. My experience with Students Without Boundaries was not the conventional experience of attendees. I didn't have the opportunity to take part in the program as a student, but rather it was in my thirties that I attended, first as an assistant leader in 2016, and then as a group leader in charge of fifty students for the duration of the program since.

I could immediately relate to these students. They were Hungarians, and in fact far more familiar with their culture and far more proficient with the language than I was, despite being more than a decade younger. We all lived in a country where we were part of a cultural minority. Like the students, I have always felt Hungarian, however, when in Hungary, I've experienced again and again that I am not considered Hungarian. Like each of the students in the program, I am a citizen and resident of a country where I do not belong to the majority. I feel 100 per cent Canadian and very proud of that; however, most Canadians think of me as being Hungarian-Canadian, emphasis on Hungarian first, with the result that I don't quite fit in here. Thus, I am at home in two cultures; but not considered part of either by others. This is an experience shared by many of the students. But there is the key area in which my experience has been very different from the students in the program; namely, in my home country, I have never experienced hatred for being different and having a second culture. This was the major difference, the shocking reality, that sunk in during my first few days of the program. This is the point that must be addressed.

Students Without Boundaries is a fantastic program, in that works to break down these historical and stereotypical barriers that exist in east-central Europe, and in many other places in the world. The program brings together young people who have had very different lives, and yet share a common heritage, as well as the experience of living in minority status. The students start to share their stories and realize within the first few days that they aren't alone in the world, that there are others from faraway places who have had similar challenges while living in minority status. The program encourages open and honest discussion about these topics, which is sadly uncommon in that part of the world. One of the major activities in the program is an evening in which students brainstorm about what it would take to make life easier and better for them while they live in minority status. This is something most have never thought of doing, even though they have experienced some level of discrimination their entire lives. The Canadian leadership in the program is particularly important, as our experience with a functional multiculturalism allows us to share a more positive side of things. I found that my critical role in the program is sharing my experiences: both those during my childhood in Canada, described above, as well as all that I have seen in my travels. Initially you see some level of skepticism in the students, but they gradually open up to the ideas and also share that they too have made baby steps forward over time, though they hadn't necessarily noticed them until they were brought to their attention.

The concept of sharing one's culture with others as an educational process, whereby we show why we are proud of who we are and where we come from, is simply foreign to many of the student participants. For them, any cultural festival would be in defiance of local rules and would simply be a show of solidarity amongst themselves. In Canada where cultural festivals are a norm, we have long ago realized that culture isn't a competition. It is not possible to convert someone to your culture; you can simply have people understand and perhaps appreciate your culture, history, customs, and famous individuals. In some rare cases, others may adopt into their own lives some aspects of your culture that they find particularly useful or intriguing, such as cuisine or folk dancing.

I have always believed that more information allows you to make better decisions in life; however, through my involvement with Students Without Boundaries, I have realized that information alone is not enough. Varied perspectives and a true appreciation and thorough processing of your past is the real key to making better and more informed decisions. Students Without Boundaries gives students the opportunity to gain some of these diverse experiences during their formative years. The students are surrounded by a group of leaders who have a broad range of experiences, both as a result of being previous participants in the program as well as having achieved something significant in their lives through their education and profession. The leaders encourage true reflection on all aspects of everyday life. This starts the students on a path to becoming leaders in their own right. These young student leaders can build on the experiences of the program, of viewing the world from a wider perspective, bringing back to their home communities the tools to help those communities become more inclusive and stronger for the future. The students who are already proud of their culture now begin to understand the culture of others. They understand each culture's unique history and strong points and the fact that, together, we can be stronger than if we simply go it alone, or engage in a bitter battle with our neighbours.

The first year that I attended Students Without Boundaries, we had a day trip to Kosice [Kassa] in Slovakia. The other leaders were weary, because in the past there have been problems with locals being angry with visiting Hungarian groups. As we walked through the centre of town, we were followed by a small group of locals who were swearing at us and telling us to go back to Hungary. The reaction in the group was to stick together, to travel through the town centre quickly, and to try and get to a safe spot inside the museum we wanted to visit. The small group however continued to shout at us from the gates of the museum. Not even the Slovakian-born students within our number were willing to say anything. It showed a cultural divide, and one that was deeply ingrained. Students had never been empowered or shown methods to try and de-escalate such situations. Fear ruled.

I later witnessed this type of cultural discrimination while on a trip through Transylvania on behalf of the Rákóczi Foundation. I boarded a train with some of our past participants, speaking in Hungarian. The train was full, so I took my assigned seat in a compartment full of Romanian students. They greeted me when I sat down, and I said "Hello," not speaking a word of Romanian myself. They tried to be friendly, but got ever more agitated that a Hungarian from the region was too proud or arrogant to learn or speak the national language. At that point, they had no way of knowing that I was not a local, but they typecast me because they had heard me speaking Hungarian as I boarded the train. It took some real effort on my part to explain I was a Hungarian-Canadian and just visiting the region before they changed back to a positive attitude toward me. It showed me how much historical stereotypes are harming the region, and also how easily honest, open communication can break down these barriers. I, too, could have done my part; I could have learned a few words in Romanian before visiting the region, a relatively easy process that could have gone a long way toward avoiding the awkward encounter I had.

These changes are difficult, and often take time. In places where borders and governments have changed so often in the past century, there is skepticism, fear, and mistrust. But positive and open experiences begin to break down these boundaries. My personal encounters across the globe have made me so much more conscious of the importance of cultural heritage, but also of the benefits of being open and learning about others. I have seen communities come together, with each nationality, each group, each individual bringing their strengths, expertise, and experiences, to make something far greater than the sum of its parts. I feel that each leader sharing these experiences at Students Without Boundaries is bringing about a change to east-central Europe, whereby a greater appreciation of neighbours, more inclusive attitudes, and open and honest dialogue is building a stronger and more sustainable community. Students Without Boundaries is helping the region to achieve its true potential, and we are developing a group of young leaders who are able to impart an inclusive, positive influence across the region, in all of Europe and beyond, now and well into the future.

András Z. Diósady

Andrew Z. Diósady was born and raised in Toronto to immigrant parents from Hungary who arrived in Canada after the 1956 revolution. He graduated from the University of Toronto's Department of Chemical Engineering with a B.Sc. in 2004 and has been a registered Professional Engineer in the province of Ontario since 2009.

Over the past fifteen years, Andrew has been responsible for the configuration and design of many large, integrated petrochemical facilities around the world. Key projects have included world-scale integrated polymer production facilities in Saudi Arabia, the U.A.E., Qatar, Kuwait, Russia, Uzbekistan, India, China, Brazil, Mexico, Canada, and the United States. He was also a lead engineer for the rebuild of two major refineries in Iraq after the second Gulf War, in addition to major refinery complexes in Ecuador, Indonesia, and the United States. Most recently, Andrew has been involved with strategic planning for the future of heavy industry, sustainability and energy transition planning, and project development for both public and private sectors in various regions across North America.

In his spare time Andrew is active in the Hungarian diaspora community and in supporting educational programs. Andrew is executive vice-president of the Rakoczi Foundation, where he works with a team of volunteers to organize events, including Students Without Boundaries, scholarship programs in both North America and Europe, and general promotion of education and Hungarian culture across the globe.

ADAPTING TO CHANGE

Karoline Farkas

As I was growing up, I realized that I was very much the type of person who would constantly push aside my own emotions about what I was going through at the time. Although it was true, I would use the excuse that someone, somewhere, had it worse than me in that moment. I chose to pretend my problems never existed, rather than see someone feel sorry for me. At the age of twenty-four, I know now that even the strongest of individuals are sometimes allowed to have bad days, to break down, and to feel bad for themselves. However; it took years to learn to face the elephant in the room, to know that ignoring a problem does not help solve the problem.

> I am lucky enough to be living in a situation where I am free to make my own decisions and express myself in the way I want others to see me.

With that said, a lot of my "problems" came with solutions. For example, when my parents got divorced, I learned coping mechanisms to accept the changes. When my mom got sick, we took her to the doctor and gave her time to heal. Or when it was time to move, again … I put my things into boxes and went on my way. Throughout all this, I had a roof over my head, food in the fridge, and support all around me. And though it may have been hard to see at that time, sometimes that is all a person needs.

That is why, in 2018, I was grateful to participate in the Rakoczi Foundation's Students Without Boundaries Program. During this time, I spent time with a bus full of fellow students, all of whom were living as minorities in their home countries. What started off as a volunteer trip turned into one of the biggest learning opportunities of my life. Within minutes of getting to know these individuals, somehow, having to park in the far lot at school, not being able to get a seat on a crowded bus, or having to buy a $300 textbook to lug around in my bag didn't seem so bad anymore.

During the first few days of camp, I was nervous about making new friends and fitting in. Not only was I still working on becoming confident when speaking Hungarian, I was also the "new" kid in a group of people who had at least one or two friends at their sides. This reminds me of one of the first memories I had with the students. We were at our first stop, Miskolc, when I came across one of the campers crying. She confided that she felt like an outcast, was homesick, and wished to return home. In that moment, I knew exactly how she felt. Between moving often, being the new kid at many schools, or even just new at this camp, I know how scary first times can be. Therefore, I understood why going home may have seemed like an easy escape from it all. At the same time, however, I knew how hard each one of these students had worked to be at this camp, and how the overall experience would be like no other. I realized that the only thing I could do to motivate her to stay was to show her that she had a friend in me. I could remind her that I was there to provide her with the support she may not have known she needed, and together we would make the most out of this adventure.

Meeting these students not only helped me grow as a person, but taught me more than any castle or museum that we visited ever could have. This was the first time I have ever had an experience like this, thus making me nervous to talk about larger issues, such as living in minority status and what it is like to live as someone you are not. However, as time went on, and I got to know them better, I learned that, in order to create awareness and come up with solutions, issues need to be confronted, large or small. Pretending something doesn't exist allows it to spiral into something bigger than it ever needed to be, thus making it harder to solve.

I also learned that I shouldn't have to hide who I am or how I feel, based on the fear of how others might react. I am lucky enough to be living in a situation where I am free to make my own decisions and express myself in the way I want others to see me, while there are many people out there, such as these students, who physically cannot be their true selves in a space that they call their home, a place where they should feel safe to be who they are, and not who someone says they should be.

Culture shock seems like the most appropriate phrase to describe how I felt during my time in Hungary and at this camp. Visiting some of

Hungary's large cities for the first time as a tourist at the age of sixteen, or even living and studying in Budapest for a year at nineteen, was nothing compared to how I felt visiting people's hometowns and learning the history of how repressed many of these students are in their own countries. After the camp ended, I was fortunate enough to stay with a fellow counsellor in her hometown in Serbia. At this point, I was aware and had learned through seeing for myself how differently people lived here compared to back home in Canada. However, what made the biggest impact, in that moment, was knowing that my own grandmother came from a little town exactly like the one my friend lived in, also in Serbia, and traded one lifestyle for another to raise a family — my family — in Canada. Comparing the two is like looking at a whole new world. To see the differences around the world truly opens a person's eyes. One does not see the large, picture-perfect postcard cities, but the towns, villages — and more importantly the people — who give them all life.

This experience not only helped me grow as a person, but changed my view on the way I see myself in the world in which I live, a world in which I am so free, yet others, my own friends, cannot say the same. Seeing the impact the work of the foundation had on these individuals, and continues to have, as I keep in touch with them now, gave me hope that I can continue to provide help to these students who know they can be more than they are now. I only hope that I can participate again in this program in the future, to continue to grow as a person, but also to change as a person and adapt to a society in a world that continues to change around me.

Karoline Farkas

Karoline Farkas was born and raised in Toronto, Canada. She is twenty-four years old. Both her parents were born in North America. Her grandparents immigrated from Hungary and the former Yugoslavia. Karoline studied Child Development for four years, receiving an honours Bachelor's degree. During this time, she also became certified to teach English as a second language, as well as spending a year in Hungary doing a course on language and cultural studies. She is now in the process of pursuing a Master's degree in the Science of Education, alongside a teaching degree, with hopes of becoming a junior elementary teacher. When she is not studying, she enjoys Hungarian folk dancing with folk-dance groups in Toronto and Kitchener, as well as working full time at an outdoor educational centre with elementary-school-aged children.

THE BITTERSWEET JOYS OF TEEN MISCOMMUNICATION

Dr. Katherine Magyarody

MY teenage experience at the Students Without Boundaries camp was characterized by miscommunication that I only understood in retrospect. However, my reckoning with this miscommunication has been vital to my understanding of my own ethnic identity and my responsibilities as a Canadian citizen to support the rights of minorities and historically marginalized groups.

The miscommunication was not literal, because my Hungarian is quite strong. Rather, despite my ability to exchange words, I learned that there were a million tiny differences between my background in the Hungarian-Canadian cultural community, the Hungarian-ness of the relatives I'd just left in Budapest, and the Hungarian-ness of my fellow campers coming from Transcarpathia in Ukraine, Transylvania in Romania, Slovakia, and Vojvodina in Serbia.

When I showed up at the Students Without Boundaries camp, I was distinctly aware that I was not the sort of "American" I thought the other campers would expect to see. I was wearing a rugby shirt from my high-school team, faded jean shorts, and Birkenstocks. I did not look as if I had appeared out of a TV teen drama or high-school comedy. Even though I was from Toronto, I thought I should be able to perform "California girl" or "New York chick" for them. Instead, the only role I could perform was "Huge Nerd" — but not the winsome type that gets a makeover before the big party. By huge, I mean both physically and metaphorically; I towered over almost everyone.

Instead, my privilege was manifest in my decision not to care about markers of traditional femininity. I only grudgingly shaved my legs. My grubbiness matched my determination to carry my massive knapsack and duffel bag up the stairs of the many school dormitories in which we stayed. This mystified the boys, who showed their respect for their female peers by carrying their luggage. In North America, such small acts of chivalry are thought to signify men's assumptions that women are helpless and in need of assistance. However, in cultures where women and girls do a huge amount of domestic labour, offers of assistance register as an offer to share their work and alleviate that burden. The boys stopped offering to help, and I felt that I'd missed some basic social courtesy. In brushing off their kindness, I belatedly realized I had lost an opportunity to make male friends, much less anything more ... zesty.

> **Students Without Boundaries was the first place that I grappled fully with the ethical demand for sensitivity in the face of my own privilege.**

Some of my friends had been to the Students Without Boundaries program and had had exciting, fleeting summer romances. There had been sneaking out! Making out! Illicit sips of alcohol! At seventeen, I had the soul of a hundred-year-old woman. I wasn't good at sneaking out, because I liked to fall asleep by 9:30. I didn't like the taste of alcohol. And I wasn't interested in kissing a boy I was probably not going to see again. After all, even if webcams already existed, what were the chances of a teen romance surviving a seven-hour time difference? Also, for the first time in my life, I had a boyfriend, a Hungarian Scout in Cleveland —who was half Croatian! How exotic! I'd already decided we would get married and have four children. This will tell you how limited my ideas of dating were at the time.

Nope. I was here to soak in the history and look around museums. (Have I mentioned I was a both an elderly teen and a Huge Nerd?)

Well, what about making friends? In North America, all the Hungarians I knew were also Scouts. We had a very definite set of shared experiences and a shared interpretation of what our culture meant to us. But I couldn't guarantee I had anything in common with these kids, even though we shared a language. It would be like assuming Kim Kardashian and Stephen Hawking would be friends because they spoke English. I was shy, and I was scared at meeting so many new kids who — according to my friends' accounts — were probably more worldly and cool than I was. I was dismayed to learn that I'd been sorted into the group with young leaders — Ildikó and Zoli were great, but I'd have been more comfortable with someone grey haired. Where was a crotchety old person I could hang out with? I could ask them a question and then just be quiet and listen and get a fond pat on the head for the attention I gave them. That was less terrifying than a bunch of people my own age with life experience and responsibility I'd probably not gain until I was thirty.

The kids were definitely more worldly and cool than I was. They were also self-possessed, intelligent, talented. When we stopped in Tokay, a zither band was playing at our restaurant, and four of them stepped up to perform an impromptu concert. And they were proud folk. Their pride didn't surprise me, but I felt an awkward churn of anxiety.

You see, in the bottom of my duffel bag was a pack of things my mother had given me to distribute to my new friends, things she thought kids might need. In her mind, the fall of communism nearly twenty years earlier hadn't brought prosperity fast enough. She packed me, amongst other things, two enormous packages of razors. But how was I going to give them away? The cool girls had definitely already got rid of their leg hair, no matter where they came from. And the set I hung out with didn't seem to need them, either.

One girl had recently been in Hungary for a tour with her dance troupe. Two others were really interested in computer programing — a decade and a half before "women in STEM" became trendy in North America. A third was fearless and wanted to travel the globe (the last I heard, she was exploring Uzbekistan). They were friendly, yes. But they were also proud and ambitious. To me, it seemed insulting to assume they were anything other than middle class, even if middle class looked different in Canada.

But I still had two packs of razors thumping around in the bottom of my duffel bag. Would I be failing in my charity ... would I be greedy ... if I didn't give them out?

On the second-last day of camp, I tried to casually mention that I had some extra razors in my bag ... if anyone wanted them? The girls in my cabin looked at me, startled. No one volunteered to take my pink Bic Silky Touch Twin Blades. They were probably wondering why, if I had razors, I hadn't used them myself. It was hideously embarrassing. So, I took them home, and they came with me to university. I used them before my Cleveland boyfriend came to visit and then dumped me.

But the thing was, that my mother hadn't been entirely wrong.

I knew there was poverty. I'd been to Erdély the year before. I'd seen the mouldering highway just disappear into mud for an inexplicable ten feet … and then begin again. I'd seen the Ceausescu-era steel mills falling apart, their concrete corpses dismembered and reassembled into village houses, and the rebars dug out and sold for scrap metal. In the shadow of a fifteenth-century castle, I'd seen farmers cutting hay by hand with scythes, as if the industrial revolution had never happened. I'd been mobbed by beggar children with patting hands as light as falling snow.

So, at camp, I just didn't think that it was my right to even hint at our material differences. To my fellow teens, it would have been offensive.

But I couldn't fail to notice that one fifteen-year-old boy had arrived in a women's button-down shirt, with his possessions in a small plastic shopping bag. He walked around barefoot, because he said it was more comfortable that way. Also, he didn't have shoes. Over the duration of the camp, he gradually appeared with proper fitting clothes, a knapsack, and sneakers. With near-magical subtlety, Zoli and Ildikó had found a way to help the boy, and I wished I had their way of offering help without bruising his hard-earned dignity.

The youngest member of our group was technically underage for the camp, with brilliant turquoise eyes and perpetually uncombed long, black hair. She wanted to be a policewoman. Ever-questioning and persistent, she attached herself like a burr to the leaders, Zoli and Ildikó, or to anyone who could patiently listen to her nonstop chatter. She came from an orphanage, and this was her holiday. The other kids were patient with her — if she was *árva* (an orphan), many of them were *félárva* (half-orphans).

I liked the barefoot boy, who was quirky and funny and wandered off from the group to look at trees. I wasn't quite sure about the little policewoman, whom I alternately pitied and found annoying in that universal little-kid way. But I didn't know how to navigate respecting my peers' right to define themselves as self-sufficient and acknowledging that I had, by accident of birth, access to far more material resources. I figured that the best thing I could do was to let go of my anxiety about playing a certain role that I thought others might want to see. Instead, I'd try to behave exactly how I would in Canada. I think I went to the camp with some sense that I was supposed to be evangelizing something, that I was supposed to represent something. And I had to let that go.

Here are some examples of me failing:

One:

Hungarians who are folksy like to sing. Across the globe, we know the same songs, what the Hungarian Scouts call the "Camp-Fire Top Forty." The kids at camp knew the same songs — but with an unexpected twist. While singing about a "yellow-legged blackbird," instead of pointing to their legs (the way I did in Canada) they pulled their eyes back for "yellow."

"You can't do that," I blurted. "It's racist!"

They smiled with indulgent incomprehension. Silly American. Only later did they understand, when I showed them pictures of my high-school friends and saw that about half of them were Asian.

"You have Chinese friends?" They might as well have been saying "space aliens."

"Of course!" I said hotly. "It's Canada. Everyone's from everywhere."

As I said it, I reflected on how different it was here, where everyone was from a specific city, town, or village. They had roots. I wish I could say that this discussion led to a deep exchange about identity and a revision of their dance moves. But I was still three years away from my course in post-colonial literature, and they were more interested in the fact that my parents' house didn't have a wall or gate around its front lawn. In this part of Europe, and even more so as you travel eastward, there are no front yards. Along the main street of a village, you walk through a corridor of whitewashed walls, punctuated by gates that lead to inner gardens and houses. In cities, the courtyards of apartment buildings are positioned away from the street. I'd never thought about what the layout of a community implied regarding our basic cultural assumptions about safety and property. I'd also never thought about the fact that I met my diverse set of friends because I commuted for an hour to get to my high school. Travelling — whether to Hungary or to Bloor and Spadina — gave me the privilege of escaping the insularity of a middle-class, mostly white, suburbia.

Two:

We were on a hike somewhere, up to a castle, when I found myself in need of a snack. I rooted around in my backpack, where I found not only that day's apple but also a three-day-old bun I thought I'd lost. I was amazed — it was hard as a rock! A fossil, in fact.

"Wow!" I said.

A girl paused at my cry. We were friendly — but not quite friends. She was one of those girls who wore high heels in all circumstances. She smiled at me, because the other day, when we'd gone to a pool, I'd tried to teach her how to swim. (The only water near where she lived was a knee-deep creek.)

I held up the bun and announced, "Look at this!" I flung the bun down onto the rocky path, where it bounced with a small dry thud.

But instead of a smile, the girl's mouth opened in shock. And then her expression ossified into contempt. "You don't treat food that way," she said. Then she turned and walked up the dusty, rocky path in her platform sandals.

I'd made a huge cultural gaffe. Food was always something I'd taken for granted. To me, the bun looked inedible. To me, that bread was not food, but an amusement, before it became garbage. And I was horribly, horribly wrong. There wasn't anything I could do. I wish I could say that I made it up to my almost-friend somehow, but I don't think I did.

Three:

We were on the bus, and I asked what special power people would want.

"What do you mean?"

"Like, would you want to be able to fly, or to breathe underwater."

"I'd want to heal people," the little policewoman said, "so they wouldn't be sick anymore."

There was a general hum of agreement. Oh man, there was nothing I could say to that.

It's strange that these are the memories that stand out most vividly. When I recently spoke to the camp's founder, Zsuzsa, she had a very different memory. During the camp, a regional representative of the

UN human-rights office gave a presentation, and during the question-and-answer period, I stood up and asked why the UN wasn't doing more for the rights of minorities living in central and eastern Europe. He asked where I was from, and expressed amazement that someone from Canada would be concerned about the rights of minorities in this region. Was he surprised that I cared, even though I wasn't "from" the region? Was he surprised that I cared, even though Canada has its own minority-rights problems? Whether I forgot my success in unnerving a UN official or remember my bumbling with my peers, however, this link between who has rights, whether "here" or "there," persists as a personal ethical concern.

Offering scholarships like the Students Without Boundaries program is a key way of helping talented young people to get where they need to go. More than this, the Students Without Boundaries program has developed the cultural capital to give teens scope for their ambitions. The program's exceptional alumni network around Europe helps teens reimagine their futures, whether it means developing their community at home or serving in the European Parliament. The great achievement of this program is that it has succeeded in building a young, vibrant leadership team based out of the Hungarian minority communities it serves.

What does this obligation mean to me as a Canadian, then and now? Students Without Boundaries was the first place that I grappled fully with the ethical demand for sensitivity in the face of my own privilege. In Canada, at that time, I wasn't ready to handle these questions. I was fifteen when an Indigenous man yelled at me at the corner of Bloor and Spadina, accusing my grandfather of stealing his land. I'd stood there, ignoring him as I waited for the traffic light to turn from a red hand to a walking white man, mentally rejecting the accusation on the basis of my grandfather's refugee status. And I'd also wondered why I was the only target of his rage, when my Vietnamese-Canadian friend was standing right beside me. I'd seen us as the same, as the descendants of refugees to an already-settled land. In the moment I was frightened, and then angry. Now, I wish I had been empathetic to the man's emotions, if not to his mode of expression. I wish I had been angry for him or with him, not at him. I hadn't yet been taught about the ways I'd benefited from systematic racism. I didn't understand that, when my grandparents fled to Canada, they were coming to a country whose colonial history granted certain benefits to immigrants — along another colonially entrenched racial hierarchy — which it denied its Indigenous peoples. In Canada, my difference was invisible and voluntary.

But, among young ethnic Hungarians who'd gathered from across the Carpathian Basin, I had no excuses. Their troubles would be my troubles. Because of the accident of birth, I was born in Canada when multiculturalism was a national ideal, and they were born to minority communities in post-imperial, post-Communist nation-states. In the borderlands, Hungarians have long lived in a mix of Romanians, Saxons, Slavs, Jews, Roma, and Armenians, among others. In the last century, the redrawing of borders to match the ideology of the nation-state made this multicultural mix increasingly fraught. Although I learned in university that Western intellectuals have declared the idea of the nation-state passé, it still has a monumental effect on the lives of these individuals.

So, if people in my ethnic community were bewailing the Trianon Treaty of 1920, then I in turn must take Indigenous land claims equally seriously. If I support or take issue with one, I must treat the other to the same process of critical thought. If I am going to support the rights of Hungarian ethnic minorities in Romania, Serbia, Slovakia, and Ukraine, then I must also educate myself about the rights of ethnic groups in Hungary, like the Roma. I must reckon equally with the difficulty of the Hungarian culture in dealing with the Holocaust. As a result, as a Hungarian Scout leader, I've shifted the way I teach history away from nineteenth-century romantic nationalism and the narrative of victimization that I learned as a child toward something more nuanced and rooted in an international context. This is a concrete step I can take to make change in a culture. And I must support the movement toward Indigenization in Canadian culture. In my Ph.D. program, this has meant researching colonial history and including Indigenous authors in the course that I taught. After academia, it has meant supporting Indigenous authors by buying, reading, and sharing their work. Since I've moved to the United States, this means shifting my focus to learning about the American context. As the mother of American citizens, I can try to imbue in my children a sense of the honour due to cultural diversity, a respect for the contingencies of place and history, and a desire to enact justice.

The Students Without Boundaries program has been vital throughout my life by providing a set of memories to which I have returned for reflection. Though I didn't understand it at the time, I felt the significance of my experiences. I am deeply grateful that the Students Without Boundaries program continues to grow, and that I was lucky enough to take part in it.

Dr. Katherine Magyarody

Katherine Magyarody is an author of young-adult fiction and an academic researcher. She is the recipient of a 2017 Robert J. Dau PEN Award for Emerging Writers and her debut novel, *The Changeling of Fenlen Forest*, was long-listed for the 2020 Sunburst Award for Excellence in Canadian Literature of the Fantastic. Her academic research centres on the representation of peer groups as a method of imperial cultural consolidation in nineteenth-century children's literature. She has published articles in *Nineteenth-Century Literature*, *Nineteenth-Century Gender Studies*, *Hungarian Studies Review*, the *Children's Literature Association Quarterly*, *Marvels and Tales: Journal of Fairy-Tale Studies*, and *The Palgrave Encyclopedia of Victorian Women's Writing*. Her reviews of contemporary children's fiction and non-fiction appear in *School Library Journal*.

THE IMPORTANCE OF RESILIENCE

Mária Horváth

Growing up in Canada, I was raised by my family to be bilingual (Hungarian and English). It seemed natural to me; something to take lightly. I was always told how lucky I was to have another language under my belt, and when I told others I not only understood Hungarian but was also fluent in it, they were in awe of me. It was not until the Students Without Boundaries Program that I realized how amazing it truly is to be a part of this community. Sure, I had been to Hungary with my family before, and marvelled at the landscape, culture, and liveliness of the country, but I never dug deep into why we Hungarians are the way we are today. I had never truly listened to the words in folk songs, which told the tales of our ancestors and the hardships they had to endure due to the Treaty of Trianon.

In the summer of 2018, I had the privilege of attending the Students Without Boundaries program. It was a well-thought-out program, designed and organized by the Rákoczi Foundation and based on love and sacrifice. Over the almost two weeks I spent in this program, I learned how important resilience is in one's life. We are not born resilient; we learn it and develop it throughout life. Without resiliency, fear and self-doubt take over one's life, and pessimism starts to set in. At the age of sixteen, I must admit, I initially had some fear and self-doubt about my abilities to fully participate in the Students Without Boundaries program, as I knew I was the only Canadian participating in the camp that year. Would the other campers think I had an odd accent? Would I be able to follow along in the songs we sang? Would I know Hungary's past as well as the others? Would I be accepted? These were all questions I had — and the answers to them all are "yes." I was made very aware of my slight Canadian accent, but I was never ridiculed for it. Yes, though it was challenging, I picked up many folk songs and joined in whenever and wherever we broke into song. It's true I did not know quite as much about our past as some of the others, but I learned so much that it made the experience well worth it. And finally, yes, everyone accepted me with open arms. As young Hungarians, we stuck together and supported one another. Many friendships bloomed, and I can say that, to this day, I am still great friends with some of the campers and keep in contact with many others!

> Meeting fellow students who were living in minority status ... changed my perspective: they helped me believe in my abilities and grow in confidence, and inspired me to reach my goals.

I had a lot of opportunities to talk to my peers on the long bus rides that took us to different historically significant and fascinating sites. Others in the program, Hungarians who lived in minority status, seemed to have the ability to bounce back and recover from setbacks and difficult experiences. Their life stories showed me that they were resilient individuals, were able to gain something from all their experiences, regardless of the outcome, and did not seem to dwell on mistakes. They could recognize the difference between circumstances that were within and outside of their control. Seeing these talented and strong people exercise resiliency helped me to focus my time and energy on what I can change, rather than wasting resources on what cannot be altered.

The presenters and guides seemed courageous, capable, and strong, and they viewed setbacks as challenges, while turning such experiences into advantages. They found ways to move on, and were motivated to try again. The lessons I learned from them help me perform better and become more resilient. They thought of themselves as survivors by accepting hardship, focusing on how to overcome difficulties, and learning what to do in the face of adversity. In fact, they seemed to be able to process their losses and grow from experiences of failure as well.

When I was much younger, I remember my father, Gabor Horvath, discussing the Treaty of Trianon and the devastation it brought to many Hungarians, but I was never quite able to comprehend the extent of this significant and historic event which was forced upon Hungarians in June of 1920. I remember being told of how the country was partitioned and of how approximately one-third of the country was all that remained, but I only recently started to understand the restrictions that came along with the treaty. Cultural and political exclusion, economic discrimination, and human-rights abuse are just some of the consequences that hundreds of thousands of Hungarians face today on the land their ancestors fought for and to which they had rights. These were all lived experiences for my fellow campers and friends, who live on the lands that were separated from Hungary.

Life often presents us with challenges. We have a choice whether to accept them and persevere, or let fear take over, feeling crushed by the changes we must make. Meeting fellow students who were living in minority status due to the devastating consequences of the Treaty of Trianon changed my perspective: they helped me believe in my abilities and grow in confidence and inspired me to reach my goals. What a tremendous opportunity to make a difference and promote wellness and resiliency in teens and cultivate a desire for giving back!

The founders and organizers of Students Without Boundaries, Béla Aykler and his wife, Zsuzsa, president of the Rakoczi Foundation, taught us, by founding this program, that anything is possible if your mind and heart are in the right place. During the past twenty-six years, an entire team of young people have become leaders and have now taken over the direction, planning, and implementation of the program. I will forever cherish my time in the Students Without Boundaries program, and one day I hope my children will have the same incredible opportunity to explore their Hungarian roots, develop their confidence and resiliency, and make worldwide friendships that will last a lifetime.

Mária Horváth

Mária Horváth was born in Ontario. She and her older brother grew up as the only Hungarian-speaking children in their town. This presented certain challenges that other children of their age did not necessarily face, like constantly translating, not having access to Hungarian phrases and language commonly used by her generation, and not being able to see relatives, since most were overseas. Maria excelled at math and art and enjoyed music and travelling, specifically visits to Hungary. She graduated early and started university at the age of sixteen, majoring in mathematics in the hopes of becoming a math teacher. Maria continues to develop her skills as an artist, and has also sold many portraits and other paintings.

BEING EMPOWERED

Mónika Borbély

In 2017, I had the honour of participating in the Students Without Boundaries program sponsored by the Rákóczi Foundation. This program consists of travelling for two weeks on a bus with a group of Hungarian students from regions outside of Hungary [Transylvania (Romania), Slovakia, Vojvodina (Serbia), and Transcarpathia (Ukraine)]. This was an entirely new experience for me, as it was truly one of the first times I had travelled to a new country by myself, let alone been put together with individuals I had never met before. I did not know what to expect, but was still optimistic, as I did have some knowledge about Hungarians living in minority status, since my grandparents and extended family still live in Transylvania, and our family had visited frequently.

Upon arrival at the program's first meeting location, Miskolc, the students were divided into two travelling groups, *Zrínyi* and *Bethlen*. The opening exercise was to put together a presentation with a creative aspect as an ice breaker, and to introduce ourselves to each other within a couple of hours. Our group, Zrínyi, decided to sing folk songs from each distinct. I felt discouraged and quite isolated at the time, as I was the only Canadian student and did not have anyone to start a conversation with or work with in a closer way. I thought I had already missed out on the very first chance to make friends. This was not the case, however, as, soon afterwards, we were able to mingle with one another and everyone was accepting, friendly, and eager to chat. Their kind behaviour only grew, and tighter bonds formed as time went on.

One of our first excursions was to visit the cave at Aggtelek. Here we were invited to the concert hall within the cave to listen to a mini concert that featured hit songs from the rock opera *István, a király*. While enjoying this concert, I was truly touched not only by the performance itself but also by how the participants interacted during the concert. I saw how deeply they resonated with the audiovisual display of their cultural background and history that was encapsulated by the surrounding acoustics and the environment. This was an initial emotional high for me during this program, and helped me realize that deeper experiences with those in my group would follow in the next two weeks.

The conversations from that point forward quickly evolved from comparing the etymological differences between *pityóka, krumpli,* or *burgonya* (all terms for the potato) to deeper discussing deeper questions about cultural differences and difficulties within their regions. With each personal story and shared laugh, I was taken aback by how resilient they are. Their ability to have fortitude, to strive to find joy and still work hard for their accomplishments, is remarkable. Meeting fellow students living in minority status made me feel empowered — empowered in the sense that they acknowledge the complexities of life but do not feel too discouraged to push against the grain. Personally, I was quite shy, so even taking the first step to travel across the Atlantic Ocean alone had made me apprehensive about the whole experience, but after these two weeks, I was reassured that there is strength in struggle. My fellow students showed me the effects people can have who are confident in their abilities to be competent, intelligent, creative, and kind. As a Canadian participating in the Students Without Boundaries program, I found that these students living in minority status had a major impact on me. They taught me that living in comfort will only hold you back, that you must look beyond fear, and that this will help you move forward. If they had not invited me in and shown compassion at the first group performance, had I not seen their self-assurance during the Aggtelek concert, I would not have understood this.

It is an understatement for me to say that I am proud to be a part of this program. But, more importantly, I have had the privilege of crossing paths with these bright students, whom I can fortunately call my friends. Because of their actions during the program, they have given me the confidence to be more open with others and be more understanding of their experiences going forward.

Mónika Borbély

Mónika Borbély is currently in her last year of undergraduate studies at York University, Glendon Campus, majoring in Environmental and Health Studies with a minor in Communications. She is a first-generation Canadian, with Transylvanian roots. She first cultivated her knowledge and appreciation of Hungarian heritage through consistent encouragement at home from her parents. Later, she became involved with institutions and programs such as the Hungarian Saturday School in Toronto and the work of the Rákóczi Foundation. In her free time, she enjoys travelling, learning languages, and folk dancing.

FINDING IDENTITY

Tamás Gáspár

Budapest

We had just said our tearful goodbyes. The 2017 Students Without Boundaries program had just wrapped up in Budapest, and for the next week I rested and wandered the city with a new connection to the country that made me smile everywhere I went. My phone buzzed ceaselessly with photos, reminding me of all the historical, cultural, and scenic destinations we visited with the program. I kept up with the conversations online, the jokes and small talk, answering the dozens of daily calls as I pursued my sightseeing, but soon the conversations outgrew these digital chats, and everyone started planning local get-togethers, conferences, and opportunities to hang out.

Unfortunately, I was not rushing off to these get-togethers, to reunite with these incredible friends I had made. Instead, I was kicking myself while I packed my bags. I had given myself a week in Budapest before I went to spend the rest of my vacation with my relatives in Slovakia. As much as I wanted to visit my friends from camp, my family was expecting me tomorrow at the train station in Győr. While I was excited to return to my father's hometown and talk with all the relatives whom I had not seen in years, I regretted not booking a longer stay, for not anticipating all these post-camp plans I would be missing.

Some of the people at camp had even written to me and extended personal invitations to their towns and cities if I ever wanted to visit. I made a spontaneous decision. Hours before I had to leave, I decided to change my travel plans dramatically, calling my family and apologetically asking if I could arrive a few days later in Slovakia, so I could visit some of my camp friends in Romania. Fortunately for me, they were very understanding, even relating a few stories of how my father had backpacked through Romania in his youth and how I would be sort of following in his footsteps. So, I changed my train ticket to Györ for a bus ticket to Sibiu and, before long, I was riding through the forested mountains of Romania.

Sibiu-Nagyszeben

In Sibiu, I was treated like part of my friend's family. I ate, slept, and helped them run errands. I even met their relatives and neighbourhood friends. It was the kind of hospitality Hungarians are known for, and it was the kind of hospitality I had always experienced back home as well. In Canada, the people you met at the Hungarian cultural centres, churches, and schools would take you into their homes without question and shower you with hospitality until *pogácsa* and *pálinka* were coming out of your ears. I was struck by how similar the behaviour and personalities of these people were to the Hungarians in my community across the pond.

What's more, in Sibiu the ratio of Hungarians to the rest of the population really resembled the numbers of Hungarians in a North American city, meaning they were in the minority. These minorities developed almost identical cultural centres, churches, and schools to the ones I had grown up working with in Canada. I was told they celebrated eclectic Hungarian holidays like Farsang, Szüret, and Locsolás in almost the exactly same way we did. The events I volunteered to help organize in Toronto were mirror images of the events these people ran, and as I viewed their home videos and family albums and heard their shared stories, I realized they, too, were hauntingly similar.

I saw myself in these people, and I suddenly felt part of something much larger. I had always seen the North American/Hungarian communities as a sort of salve or Band-Aid for the 1956 refugees. They missed their homes, so they created little pockets of home wherever they were. I saw clear evidence of this homesickness when these communities would close up shop in the summer, since so many Hungarian-Canadians took their vacations "back home," in Hungary. All of this seemed completely obvious — 'Hungarians are Hungarians, so of course they do the same things' — but what was shocking to me was that, here in Sibiu, I was seeing a carbon copy of what we had back home, though Hungary proper was a mere day's drive away. This was the beginning of a much larger realization, that I only truly figured out days later, after a little more travelling.

Transfăgărășan-Transzfogaras

The rest of my time in Sibiu was spent viewing the beauty of the region and city. My friend from camp took me biking with his siblings through the gothic town square, and we went swimming in the salty hot springs. On those days I felt a little like I was back at the Students Without Boundaries program, travelling around, taking in the architecture and natural beauty and discovering something new and fantastic, though what I was shown on my last day was unlike anything I had seen before, and still remains one of the most beautiful places I have ever seen. We embarked on a family road trip, with everyone crammed into the car, and a few siblings even sitting in the trunk. As we gained altitude and saw more and more of the world outside, the closeness of the car ride faded away and the open air of the mountains filled our senses. This was the Transfăgărășan.

The ascent was by a winding road, where each turn climbed above the rooftops of towns and villages, then above the treeline, then above the clouds. The roads were made slick by these clouds that swam next to us like whales and sometimes swallowed cars and motorcycles whole. Our driver, my friend's father, suddenly pulled over to the side of the road; nature was calling. We all unbuckled to stretch our legs, but when I opened the door on my side, a sheer ninety-degree drop greeted me, with adrenaline and vertigo. All of us exited safely on the opposite side and investigated a small monument that was off to the side of the road.

The modest statue, made of jagged rocks, had a plaque that told the story of this road's construction as a radical project by a radical government attempting to protect itself militarily with a strategic mountain pass. On one hand, the monument tells the story of what happens when untrained workers are met with millions of kilograms of dynamite. The project was estimated to have cost hundreds of lives, but the precise numbers are unknown. On the other hand, the story is a more familiar one, one that I had learned just weeks ago at the Rákoczi camp. This monument told the story of everyday people caught up in the conflict of giants, the real victims of political strife and warfare, who haunt their territories for generations. I wondered how many of my loved ones back home might have been buried under this mountain had they not escaped, had they not fled.

Lake Bâlea-Bilea-tó

The final stretch of the road emerged from the forest onto a sloping meadow. Sheepherders slowed our ascent with their crossing flocks and gave us plenty of time to admire the view. Rushing mountain streams flowed under and around the slithering road we had diligently climbed. At the summit, we reached Lake Bâlea. The water was bluer than the sky, and when I suggested we go for a swim, I was dared to dip my feet in. It was like ice, but ironically the water's frigid temperature reminded me of Ontario's northern lakes, and I realized something: being here felt like being at home.

Unlike the other sixty attendees of the Students Without Boundaries program, I was born in Canada, which meant that, while I shared with them a language, ethnicity, and culinary obsession with paprika, I also had an alternate cultural identity. I love Canada for its natural beauty, and I cannot imagine myself not spending the seasons out in the wilderness canoeing, tobogganing, and smiling at red maple leaves. While I have painted a mostly joyful picture of the program, there were also many serious and somber conversations. Students shared their personal and local stories of prejudice and resistance and many of these stories left me wondering about my own identity. Until then, I was not sure if, in the face of oppression, I would cling to my Hungarian identity as bravely as these students had.

However, when I asked myself what I would do if I were forced to leave Canada because of war or political conflict, I had the answer. I would take my Canadian identity with me no matter where I went, I would spend my seasons in the wilderness, just as I was doing here in Romania. And, as I was called back to the car by my friend from Sibiu, I realized I would take what they had given me too, my Hungarian identity, including the hospitality toward strangers, the organized community gatherings, and, most importantly, the pursuit of beauty as a source of truth.

Tamás Gáspár

Tamás was born in 1996 in Canada. His mother was also born in Canada, but his father was born in Czechoslovakia. At home, the family speaks an organic mix of English and Hungarian, blending vocabulary and grammar — sometimes for the funniest results. He shares a passion for arts and crafts with his mother. Tamás also has a younger brother with whom he enjoys travelling; they share a childlike optimism about people and the world.

    Tamás volunteers with Hungarian-Canadian organizations in Toronto: schools, churches, community centres, folk-dance groups, summer camps, and charities. These groups have taught him how to work with others and how to foster community. After almost a decade, these groups have become a part of his life. He cannot imagine a future in which he is not fostering, sustaining, or creating community somewhere in the world. Whenever he has some free time, Tamás enjoys creative activities like drawing, making music, and writing stories. He has always enjoyed a movie or book that makes his heart hurt or brings tears to his eyes. One day he hopes to write his own story. Tamás completed a Bachelor's degree in literature and hopes to help young people discover the power of writing as a teacher.

ACKNOWLEDGEMENTS

Dr. Susan M. Papp

THIS volume was made possible by the dedicated efforts of many individuals already listed in the Preface. However, a special thanks is extended to Katalin Kálmán Hajdók and Zoltán Csadi, who helped to read and assess more than 90 submissions that were received in response to the call for essays.

Katalin Kálmán Hajdók was born in Prague. She was nine years old when the independent Slovak Republic was established in 1993 and she experienced first-hand the significant changes in her social environment. Ms. Kálmán Hajdók received her master's degree in economics and management from the Agricultural University in Nitra, Slovakia. Her most recent position was with IBM Slovakia as Education Manager, focused on talent development and cross team collaboration. She has been involved with the work of the Foundation since the age of fifteen.

Zoltán Csadi is an actor and artistic director of the Bartók Theatre in Hungary. In addition, he is pursuing a doctorate degree in theatre arts and the history of Hungarian theatre at the Eötvös Loránd University in Budapest. He was born and raised in Feketenyék (Cierna Voda), a small village in Slovakia. Zoltán believes the work of the Foundation is key to peaceful coexistence in east-central Europe. He is Executive Director of the II. Rákóczi Ferenc Foundation in Budapest.

Special thanks also goes to the dedicated work of the translators of this volume, Peter Csermely, who translated the original essays from Hungarian to English, and Mária Máté, who translated the Canadian submissions along with the Preface and Introduction, into Hungarian. Their work made it possible for this volume of essays to be published separately in English and Hungarian, in order to reach a much wider audience.

www.ingramcontent.com/pod-product-compliance
Lightning Source LLC
Chambersburg PA
CBHW050741080526
44579CB00018B/126